INCREDIBLE ANIMAL FACTS AND TRIVIA FOR KIDS

Fascinating facts for kids About World's Most
Incredible Creatures

By

Eli Spark

Table of Content

Introduction

Get ready for an exciting adventure into the wildest, weirdest, and most wonderful world of animals! From the giants of the deep sea to tiny creatures with incredible strength, this book will take you on a journey through some of nature's most amazing secrets. You'll discover facts that will make you say "Wow!" as you explore the fantastic lives of creatures big and small.

Have you ever wondered how fast a cheetah can run, or how an octopus changes its color? How about animals with superpowers, like those that can grow back lost limbs or glow in the dark? This book is packed with incredible facts and stories that will spark your curiosity and make you look at the animal kingdom in a whole new way.

So, grab your imagination and let's dive into the wild! Whether you're learning about camouflage experts, animal communication, or the fastest speedsters on the planet, you're in for an amazing ride full of jaw-dropping discoveries. Let's explore the animal world together!

The Giants of the Animal Kingdom

The Largest Animals On Earth

Let's take a look at the *biggest* animals that have roamed or are currently roaming our planet. From the tallest land animals to the largest creatures of the sea, these giants will blow your mind with their size and amazing abilities!

❖ **What is the largest animal ever to live on Earth?**
The blue whale holds this title! A blue whale can grow up to 100 feet long (which is about the size of two school buses parked end to end!) and can weigh as much as 400,000 pounds. Its heart alone is the size of a small car, and it eats up to 8,000 pounds of krill a day!

❖ **Which bird has the largest wingspan?**
The wandering albatross has the largest wingspan of any bird, stretching up to 12 feet from tip to tip. These birds can glide for hours without flapping their wings and travel thousands of miles over the open ocean!

❖ **What's the tallest land animal?**
The giraffe takes this title, reaching heights of up to 18 feet! That's taller than most two-story houses. A giraffe's neck alone can be 6 feet long, which helps them reach high branches to munch on leaves.

❖ **Which animal lays the largest egg?**
The ostrich lays the biggest eggs of any bird, with each egg weighing about 3 pounds and being about the size of a small melon. Ostriches are also the largest birds on Earth, standing up to 9 feet tall!

❖ **What's the heaviest land mammal?**
The African elephant is the heaviest land animal, weighing up to 14,000 pounds (that's as heavy as two large cars!). These gentle

giants use their massive size to push through dense forests and defend themselves from predators.

❖ How big can an anaconda get?

The green anaconda is one of the heaviest and longest snakes in the world. It can grow up to 30 feet long and weigh more than 500 pounds! These snakes live in South America's rainforests and are powerful swimmers.

❖ Which animal has the largest brain?

The sperm whale holds the record for the largest brain of any animal. Its brain weighs about 17 pounds, which is more than five times the size of a human brain! Sperm whales use their intelligence to communicate with complex clicks and sounds.

❖ What's the biggest fish in the world?

The whale shark is the largest fish, growing up to 40 feet long and weighing as much as 20 tons! Despite their enormous size, whale sharks are gentle and feed mainly on tiny plankton.

❖ Which animal has the biggest claws?

The giant armadillo has the longest claws of any mammal, with some claws reaching up to 8 inches long. These claws help the armadillo dig deep burrows and search for insects underground.

❖ What's the largest land carnivore?

The polar bear is the largest land carnivore, with males weighing up to 1,500 pounds. These powerful hunters use their size to catch seals, which make up most of their diet.

Fun Fact Quiz

Which of these animals holds the title for the largest animal ever to live on Earth?

A. African Elephant
B. Blue Whale
C. Giraffe
D. Whale Shark

Answer
B. Blue Whale

The blue whale is the largest animal to have ever lived on Earth. Growing up to 100 feet long and weighing as much as 400,000 pounds, these ocean giants are truly remarkable. A blue whale's heart is the size of a small car, and they consume up to 8,000 pounds of krill each day!

Land Giants

Now that we've explored some of the biggest animals overall, let's take a closer look at the giants of the land. These creatures are not only massive in size, but they also have some pretty cool adaptations that make them true survivors.

❖ **Why do giraffes have long necks?**
Giraffes evolved long necks to help them reach leaves at the tops of trees that other animals can't get to. This gives them a major advantage when food is scarce. Their necks also help them spot predators from far away.

❖ **How strong is an elephant's trunk?**
An elephant's trunk is one of the most amazing tools in the animal kingdom. It has over 40,000 muscles (compare that to the 600 muscles in a human body!). Elephants use their trunks to grab food, drink water, and even as a snorkel when swimming!

❖ **What's the longest land animal?**
The reticulated python is the longest land animal, growing up to 30 feet in length. Unlike some snakes, pythons don't have venom. Instead, they use their muscular bodies to squeeze their prey.

❖ **Can an elephant jump?**
No, elephants are one of the few animals that can't jump! Their large size and weight make jumping impossible, but they can still run at speeds of 25 miles per hour to escape danger.

❖ **How does a rhino protect itself?**
Rhinos have thick skin that acts like armor and a horn that they use for defense. Some species, like the white rhino, can weigh up to 5,000 pounds, making them one of the heaviest land animals.

❖ **How do camels survive in the desert?**

Camels are perfectly adapted for life in the desert. Their humps store fat (not water!) that they can use for energy when food is scarce. They can also go for days without drinking water, and when they do drink, they can gulp down up to 40 gallons at once!

❖ **What's the largest herbivore on land?**

The African elephant is the largest herbivore, and it needs to eat a lot to sustain its massive size—about 300 pounds of food every day! Elephants use their trunks and tusks to strip bark off trees and pull down branches.

❖ **How do giraffes sleep?**

Giraffes have to be careful when sleeping because they're vulnerable to predators. They only sleep for short periods, usually standing up. When they do lie down, they tuck their legs under them and rest their heads on their backs.

❖ **What's special about a bison's hump?**

The American bison has a large hump on its shoulders that's made of muscle. This helps it plow through deep snow during the winter and dig for grass underneath.

Fun Fact Quiz

Why do giraffes have long necks?

A. To help them run faster
B. To help them reach high leaves
C. To help them breathe better
D. To make them taller than other animals

Answer
B. To help them reach high leaves

Giraffes evolved long necks so they could reach leaves at the tops of trees, giving them an advantage when food is scarce. This unique adaptation also helps them spot predators from afar, making it a vital survival feature in the wild!

Ocean Behemoths

Let's dive into the depths of the ocean to meet some of the largest and most mysterious creatures living in the sea. From enormous squids to gentle giants like the whale shark, the ocean is full of fascinating animals that will leave you in awe.

❖ **How big is the colossal squid?**
The colossal squid is one of the largest invertebrates on Earth. It can grow up to 45 feet long and has massive eyes, some of the largest in the animal kingdom, which help it see in the dark depths of the ocean.

❖ **What's the largest shark?**
The whale shark is the biggest shark in the ocean. It can grow to be over 40 feet long, but don't worry, it's not dangerous to humans. Whale sharks are filter feeders and eat tiny plankton and small fish.

❖ **Can a blue whale really weigh as much as 33 elephants?**
Yes! The blue whale is not only the largest animal ever to live on Earth, but it can also weigh up to 400,000 pounds, which is the equivalent of about 33 elephants!

❖ **What's the largest jellyfish?**
The lion's mane jellyfish has the longest tentacles of any jellyfish, reaching up to 120 feet! That's longer than a blue whale. These tentacles are covered in stinging cells used to catch prey.

❖ **How deep can a sperm whale dive?**
Sperm whales are expert divers, plunging to depths of over 7,000 feet in search of their favorite food: giant squid. They can hold their breath for up to 90 minutes while hunting.

❖ **What's the heaviest bony fish?**
The ocean sunfish holds this record, weighing up to 5,000 pounds.

These odd-looking fish have flat bodies and can grow to be 10 feet across. Despite their size, they feed mostly on jellyfish.

❖ What's the fastest fish in the ocean?

The black marlin is one of the fastest swimmers in the ocean, capable of reaching speeds of up to 82 miles per hour! They use their speed to catch smaller fish like tuna.

❖ What's the biggest carnivore in the ocean?

The orca, also known as the killer whale, is the largest ocean carnivore. Orcas can weigh up to 12,000 pounds and are at the top of the food chain. They're highly social and hunt in packs, like wolves of the sea.

❖ How does a humpback whale sing?

Male humpback whales are known for their beautiful and complex songs, which can last up to 30 minutes and be heard miles away. These songs are thought to help them attract mates.

❖ What's the largest animal with tentacles?

The giant Pacific octopus has the longest arms of any octopus, stretching up to 16 feet. They use their strong, flexible arms to catch prey and defend themselves from predators.

Fun Fact Quiz

What is the largest shark in the ocean?

A. Great White Shark
B. Tiger Shark
C. Whale Shark
D. Hammerhead Shark

Answer
C. Whale Shark

The whale shark is the largest shark in the ocean, reaching lengths of over 40 feet! Despite their massive size, whale sharks are gentle giants that feed mainly on plankton and small fish. They pose no threat to humans, as they are filter feeders and have no interest in large prey.

Tiny Titans:
Small But Mighty Animals

Incredible Insects

Did you know that insects are some of the most diverse and **fascinating creatures** on Earth? Though they're tiny, they're capable of doing things that would blow your mind! Let's dive into some **fun facts** about these amazing insects.

❖ **Did you know ants can carry objects 50 times their own body weight?**
That's like a human lifting a car! Ants use their incredible strength to carry food, build their nests, and even fight off predators.

❖ **What insect is the strongest in the world?**
The dung beetle takes the crown for the strongest insect. It can pull objects that are over 1,000 times its own weight—this would be like a person pulling six double-decker buses!

❖ **Can a cockroach really survive a nuclear explosion?**
Cockroaches are incredibly tough and can survive extreme conditions, but they wouldn't survive a nuclear explosion. However, they can live for up to a week without their heads and survive on almost anything, even glue!

❖ **What insect has the fastest punch?**
The mantis shrimp has a punch so fast and powerful that it can break the glass of an aquarium! Its punch is delivered at 50 miles per hour, and it creates shockwaves in the water that stun its prey.

❖ **How long can a termite queen live?**
The termite queen can live for up to 50 years, making her one of the longest-living insects in the world! During her lifetime, she lays millions of eggs to keep her colony thriving.

❖ **Can bees recognize human faces?**
Yes! Honeybees are surprisingly smart and can recognize human

faces. They use this skill to remember which humans are friendly and which might be a threat.

❖ What's the loudest insect in the world?

The cicada holds the record for the loudest insect. Some species can produce sounds up to 120 decibels—that's as loud as a rock concert!

❖ Did you know that fireflies aren't really flies?

Fireflies are actually beetles! They use chemicals in their bodies to produce light, which they flash to communicate with each other, attract mates, and even ward off predators.

❖ What insect can survive freezing temperatures?

The antarctic midge is a tiny insect that can survive in the freezing conditions of Antarctica. It's so tough that it can lose up to 70% of its body water and still survive being frozen for months!

❖ How many eyes does a dragonfly have?

A dragonfly has up to 30,000 lenses in each of its two huge eyes! This allows it to see in almost every direction and makes it one of the most effective hunters in the insect world.

❖ Did you know that butterflies taste with their feet?

Butterflies have taste sensors on their feet, which they use to check if a plant is good for laying their eggs. If the plant tastes right, they'll lay their eggs on it so their babies can eat it when they hatch!

❖ What insect has the longest lifespan?

Termites have one of the longest lifespans among insects. A termite queen can live up to 50 years, continuing to produce eggs throughout her life!

❖ Can ants really farm?

Some ants, like leafcutter ants, are known as "farmers" because they cut leaves and bring them back to their nests to grow fungus. The ants eat this fungus, making them true farmers of the insect world!

❖ What's the fastest flying insect?

The dragonfly holds the title for the fastest flying insect, reaching speeds of up to 35 miles per hour. Its incredible flying skills help it catch other insects in mid-air.

❖ Do all beetles fly?

Many beetles can fly, but some, like the ground beetle, have lost their ability to fly over time. These beetles rely on their speed to escape predators instead of taking to the air.

❖ How long do cicadas live underground?

Some species of cicadas spend up to 17 years underground as larvae before emerging as adults. When they finally come out, they live for only a few weeks to mate and lay eggs.

❖ What's the smallest insect in the world?

The fairyfly is the smallest insect on Earth, measuring only 0.5 millimeters long. You'd need a microscope to see it clearly!

❖ Can a tarantula live longer than a dog?

Yes, female tarantulas can live up to 30 years in the wild! That's longer than many household pets like cats and dogs.

❖ How many species of insects are there?

There are an estimated 10 million species of insects on Earth, making them the most diverse group of animals. Scientists are discovering new species all the time!

Fun Fact Quiz

What is the strongest insect in the world?

A. Ant
B. Dung Beetle
C. Honeybee
D. Dragonfly

Answer
B. Dung Beetle

The dung beetle is the strongest insect, capable of pulling objects over 1,000 times its own weight—like a person pulling six double-decker buses!

Mini Mammals

Even though we tend to think of mammals as larger animals like dogs, cats, or elephants, some mammals are **incredibly tiny**. Let's meet some of the smallest but most fascinating mammals on the planet!

❖ What's the tiniest mammal on Earth?
The bumblebee bat holds this title, weighing less than a penny and measuring only about 1 inch long. These bats are small, but they can fly as fast as larger bats, catching tiny insects for food.

❖ How does the pygmy shrew survive?
The pygmy shrew is one of the smallest mammals, weighing only 2 grams. Despite its tiny size, it has to eat almost constantly to stay alive, consuming up to twice its own body weight in food every day!

❖ What's the smallest monkey?
The pygmy marmoset is the world's tiniest monkey, weighing about 4 ounces and standing 6 inches tall. These little monkeys live in the rainforests of South America and are known for their high-pitched calls.

❖ How does the Etruscan shrew stay warm?
The Etruscan shrew has one of the fastest metabolisms of any mammal. To stay warm, it has to eat nearly constantly, consuming insects and small animals. Its heart beats up to 1,500 times per minute!

❖ Why is the fennec fox's fur so important?
The fennec fox is the smallest fox species, but its large ears and thick fur help it survive in the hot desert. Its fur reflects heat during the day and keeps it warm during the cold nights.

❖ What's the smallest rodent?

The African pygmy mouse is the smallest rodent, measuring just 2 to 3 inches long. Despite its tiny size, it can jump as high as 12 inches in the air to escape predators!

❖ Do tiny bats sleep upside down?

Yes! Pipistrelle bats, one of the smallest bat species, sleep upside down just like their larger relatives. They weigh only 5 grams but are great at catching insects in the air.

❖ How far can the tiny jumping mouse leap?

The kangaroo rat might be tiny, but it can jump 9 feet in one leap! This helps it escape from predators in the deserts of North America.

❖ What's special about the least weasel?

The least weasel is the smallest member of the weasel family, measuring 7 to 8 inches long. Despite its small size, it's a fierce hunter and can take down prey much larger than itself!

❖ Why do pygmy possums hibernate?

The pygmy possum hibernates during the cold winter months to conserve energy. This tiny marsupial curls up into a ball and lowers its body temperature to survive the cold.

❖ What's the smallest carnivorous mammal?

The pygmy shrew is the smallest carnivorous mammal, feeding on insects, spiders, and small animals. It needs to eat almost constantly to maintain its energy levels.

❖ Do all small mammals live in warm climates?

No! Some small mammals, like the arctic shrew, live in cold environments and have adapted to survive by burrowing under the snow to keep warm.

❖ **Can a dormouse really sleep for six months?**
Yes! The common dormouse hibernates for up to six months during the winter, conserving energy until food becomes available in the spring.

❖ **What's the smallest mammal that can glide?**
The sugar glider is a tiny marsupial that can glide through the air by spreading out a membrane between its limbs. They can glide distances of 150 feet from tree to tree!

❖ **How small is the American pygmy shrew?**
The American pygmy shrew weighs less than a dime and is only 3 inches long. It has an incredibly fast metabolism and needs to eat constantly to survive.

❖ **Can a tiny mouse have a big voice?**
The singing vole is a small rodent that "sings" to communicate with other voles. They make high-pitched calls to warn each other of danger.

❖ **What's the smallest species of deer?**
The pudu is the smallest deer species in the world, standing just 14 inches tall at the shoulder. It lives in the forests of South America and is known for its ability to blend into its environment.

❖ **Why do small animals often have short lifespans?**
Tiny mammals like the pygmy shrew have short lifespans because their fast metabolisms wear their bodies out quickly. While larger mammals may live for decades, these small creatures often only live for 1 to 2 years.

❖ **What's the smallest bear species?**
The sun bear is the smallest bear, standing only about 4 feet tall. Despite its small size, it's known for its long tongue, which it uses to extract honey from beehives.

Fun Fact Quiz

What is the tiniest mammal on Earth?

A. Pygmy shrew
B. Bumblebee bat
C. African pygmy mouse
D. Pipistrelle bat

Answer
B. Bumblebee bat

The bumblebee bat is the tiniest mammal, weighing less than a penny and measuring only about 1 inch long!

Tiniest Reptiles & Amphibians

Even among reptiles and amphibians, there are some **tiny titans** that play important roles in their ecosystems. Let's learn about these small but mighty creatures!

❖ **Did you know that some lizards can fit on your fingertip?**
The nano-chameleon is the smallest lizard in the world, measuring less than 1 inch long. These tiny reptiles are found in Madagascar and are so small they can fit on the tip of your finger!

❖ **What's the smallest frog in the world?**
The Paedophryne amauensis frog is the tiniest frog, measuring only 0.3 inches. These frogs are so small that they can sit on a penny!

❖ **Can tiny frogs be poisonous?**
Yes! The golden poison dart frog is one of the most toxic animals on Earth, despite being only about 1 inch long. Just one of these frogs contains enough poison to kill 10 adult humans.

❖ **Why do some reptiles and amphibians have bright colors?**
Tiny amphibians like the strawberry poison dart frog have bright colors to warn predators that they are poisonous. Their bright red bodies stand out in the green jungle to keep predators away.

❖ **Do all small reptiles live in warm climates?**
While many small reptiles live in tropical areas, some, like the common gecko, can survive in cooler climates by hiding in warm crevices or burrowing underground.

❖ **Can a chameleon really change color?**
Yes, the Brookesia micra, one of the smallest chameleons, can change its color to blend into its surroundings. This tiny chameleon is about the size of a paperclip!

❖ **How small is the world's tiniest snake?**
The Barbados threadsnake is the smallest snake in the world, measuring only 4 inches long. This tiny reptile lives in the Caribbean and feeds on insects and small spiders.

❖ **What's the smallest species of turtle?**
The speckled padloper tortoise is the tiniest turtle, measuring only about 4 inches long. It's found in South Africa and is known for its colorful, speckled shell.

❖ **How do tiny frogs avoid being eaten?**
Many small frogs, like the Amazon milk frog, use their colorful patterns to blend into their surroundings, making it hard for predators to spot them.

❖ **Do tiny reptiles have big appetites?**
Despite their size, some tiny reptiles like the Mediterranean house gecko have big appetites and can eat hundreds of insects every day!

❖ **Can a small reptile be a fast runner?**
Yes! The western fence lizard, which is only about 3 inches long, can run up to 15 miles per hour to escape predators.

❖ **Why are some small amphibians transparent?**
The glass frog has see-through skin, which helps it blend into its surroundings. These tiny frogs are found in the rainforests of Central and South America.

❖ **What's the smallest salamander?**
The minute salamander is the tiniest salamander, measuring just 1 inch long. These small amphibians are found in Mexico and Central America, where they live in leaf litter and under logs.

❖ **How do tiny reptiles keep warm?**
Many small reptiles, like the pygmy gecko, rely on the sun to keep

warm. They bask on rocks and leaves during the day and retreat to cool, shady spots when it gets too hot.

❖ Can a tiny amphibian be a great jumper?

Yes! The Amazonian rocket frog may be small, but it can jump over 6 feet in one leap to escape predators!

❖ How do small reptiles protect themselves from predators?

Tiny reptiles like the anole lizard have special adaptations like camouflage and the ability to detach their tails to escape predators.

❖ Do all small amphibians live in water?

While many amphibians start their lives in water, some, like the red-eyed tree frog, live in trees and only return to water to lay their eggs.

❖ How do tiny frogs communicate?

Small frogs like the Coqui frog use loud calls to communicate with each other. Despite being only 1.5 inches long, their calls can be heard from miles away.

❖ Can small reptiles live in the desert?

Yes! The desert banded gecko is a tiny lizard that lives in the desert. It uses its small size to hide under rocks and in burrows to escape the scorching sun.

These **tiny titans** of the animal kingdom may be small, but they've evolved amazing abilities to thrive in their environments. From the strength of ants to the poison of dart frogs, these animals show that **size doesn't determine power!**

Fun Fact Quiz

What is the smallest snake in the world?

A. Garden Snake
B. Barbados Threadsnake
C. Garter Snake
D. Coral Snake

Answer
B. Barbados Threadsnake

The Barbados threadsnake measures only 4 inches long, making it the smallest snake in the world. This tiny reptile can be found in the Caribbean, where it feeds on insects and small spiders, showcasing that even the smallest creatures can have significant roles in their ecosystems!

Masters of Camouflage and Mimicry

Color-Changing Creatures

Animals have some incredible abilities when it comes to blending in with their surroundings. Some can even **change color** to disappear! Let's dive into the amazing world of color-changing animals.

❖ **Did you know chameleons change color to talk to each other?**
Chameleons aren't just changing color to hide; they use their shifting skin tones to communicate their mood. If they're angry, their skin may turn a darker color!

❖ **Can octopuses change their color in an instant?**
Yes! The common octopus can change its color and texture in less than a second. It uses this ability to blend into coral, rocks, or sand, making it almost impossible to see.

❖ **Do some fish change color too?**
The cuttlefish is a master of color-changing. It can change its skin color, pattern, and even texture to match its surroundings or communicate with other cuttlefish.

❖ **How do squids use color to confuse predators?**
Squids, like the Humboldt squid, can flash different colors to confuse predators and slip away unnoticed in the ocean's depths.

❖ **What's the trick behind a chameleon's color change?**
A chameleon changes color by adjusting special cells called chromatophores in its skin. These cells contain different pigments that reflect light in various ways.

❖ **Can some animals change colors with the seasons?**
The arctic hare has white fur in the winter to blend in with the snow

and brown fur in the summer to blend in with the tundra. This helps them stay hidden all year round!

❖ Did you know sea horses can blend in too?
The leafy sea dragon is so good at changing color, it looks just like a piece of seaweed swaying in the ocean, fooling both prey and predators.

❖ Can frogs change color?
Some frogs, like the European tree frog, can change from bright green to dark brown depending on the temperature, light, and their mood.

❖ What animal uses color-changing to hunt prey?
The banded sea krait is a snake that changes the color of its bands from bright yellow to dull gray, confusing its prey as it hunts.

❖ Do reptiles other than chameleons change color?
Yes! The anole lizard can also change colors from bright green to brown, helping it blend in with trees or the forest floor.

❖ Can an octopus look like a rock?
The mimic octopus can flatten its body and take on the appearance of a rock or coral. It can even copy the behavior of other sea creatures like flatfish!

❖ Why do squid use light to blend in?
Some deep-sea squids, like the firefly squid, use bioluminescence to blend in with the faint light filtering down from the surface. This helps them become nearly invisible to predators from below.

❖ How do lizards use light to their advantage?
The mourning gecko uses the light around it to change its color. In bright sunlight, it turns pale to reflect heat, and in shadows, it darkens to stay hidden.

❖ **Can a chameleon turn blue?**

While chameleons are often associated with green or brown, some species, like the panther chameleon, can turn bright blue when they are excited or trying to attract a mate.

❖ **Did you know squid can hypnotize prey?**

The bobtail squid has light-producing bacteria in its body that create a glowing effect, helping it camouflage itself in moonlit waters and confuse prey.

❖ **Can sea stars change color too?**

Yes! The crown-of-thorns sea star can change color from purple to red or brown to blend into the coral it hides among.

❖ **Do jellyfish use color-changing too?**

The Atolla jellyfish uses a trick called a "burglar alarm," where it lights up in a glowing blue ring when attacked, startling predators long enough for it to escape.

❖ **Why do some color-changers glow in the dark?**

Animals like the glow worm or anglerfish use bioluminescence to not only blend into their surroundings but also to lure prey closer, using light as bait.

❖ **Can chameleons stay one color for long?**

While chameleons are famous for their color changes, they usually stay a specific shade when relaxed, such as a neutral green or brown, to save energy.

Fun Fact Quiz

What ability allows a common octopus to blend into its surroundings?

A. Bioluminescence
B. Color and texture change
C. Camouflage
D. Body temperature regulation

Answer
B. Color and texture change

The common octopus can change both its color and texture in less than a second, allowing it to blend seamlessly into coral, rocks, or sand. This incredible ability makes it nearly invisible to predators and prey alike, showcasing the amazing adaptations of color-changing creatures!

Masters Of Disguise

Some animals take camouflage to the next level by perfectly **mimicking** their environment. These creatures don't just change color—they shape themselves to look exactly like their surroundings!

❖ **Did you know insects can look like sticks?**
The stick insect is one of the most famous masters of disguise. It looks just like a twig, so predators often overlook it when they're hunting for food.

❖ **Can fish really look like plants?**
The leaf scorpionfish perfectly mimics dead leaves floating in the water, allowing it to sneak up on prey without being noticed.

❖ **Is there a lizard that looks like a leaf?**
Yes! The Satanic leaf-tailed gecko from Madagascar looks exactly like a dead leaf, complete with veins and edges, helping it hide in the forest.

❖ **Why do some caterpillars mimic bird droppings?**
Some caterpillars, like the swallowtail caterpillar, disguise themselves as bird droppings to avoid being eaten by predators. It's a gross but effective strategy!

❖ **Did you know there's a spider that looks like a flower?**
The crab spider can mimic the petals of flowers, waiting for unsuspecting pollinators like bees and butterflies to land close enough for it to catch.

❖ **Can frogs disguise themselves as rocks?**
The Vietnamese mossy frog has a bumpy, green-and-brown skin that makes it look just like a clump of moss, perfect for hiding in wet forests.

❖ **What insect looks like a piece of bark?**
The bark mantis blends in so well with tree bark that predators pass by without noticing it. It also uses its disguise to ambush its prey.

❖ **Can butterflies blend into the forest?**
The dead leaf butterfly has wings that look exactly like a dried-up leaf when they are closed, making it almost invisible when it rests on the forest floor.

❖ **Why do octopuses mimic other animals?**
The mimic octopus doesn't just blend in—it can copy the shapes and movements of dangerous animals like lionfish or sea snakes, scaring off predators!

❖ **Is there a fish that pretends to be a rock?**
The stonefish is one of the best at disguise. It looks like a rock or coral, making it hard for both prey and predators to spot.

❖ **Did you know crabs can wear seaweed?**
The decorator crab picks up seaweed, sponges, and shells to stick on its back, blending into its surroundings to avoid predators.

❖ **Can birds use disguise too?**
The common potoo is a bird that looks just like a broken tree branch when it sits still. Its feathers match the bark perfectly!

❖ **Can a lizard really disappear into sand?**
The horned lizard can bury itself in the sand, leaving only its eyes visible, allowing it to hide from predators in the desert.

❖ **How do snakes disguise themselves?**
The Gaboon viper has a pattern on its scales that mimics dead leaves, allowing it to stay hidden in the undergrowth as it waits for prey.

❖ **Can beetles look like poop?**
The tortoise beetle has a shiny shell that can reflect light to look like bird droppings, keeping it safe from hungry birds.

❖ **What animal looks like a pile of sand?**
The stargazer fish buries itself in the sand with only its eyes and mouth showing. It waits there to ambush prey as it swims by.

Fun Fact Quiz

Which of the following animals can mimic the appearance of a dead leaf?

A. Stick insect
B. Satanic leaf-tailed gecko
C. Dead leaf butterfly
D. Leaf scorpionfish

Answer
B. Satanic leaf-tailed gecko

The Satanic leaf-tailed gecko from Madagascar is a master of disguise, perfectly mimicking a dead leaf, including its veins and edges. This incredible camouflage helps it hide from predators in the forest!

Why Do Animals Use Camouflage?

Camouflage helps animals survive in the wild. But have you ever wondered **why** they use these amazing tricks? Here's a look at how animals use camouflage for hunting, defense, and even social interactions!

❖ **Did you know animals use camouflage to avoid predators?**
Many animals, like the leaf-tailed gecko, use camouflage to hide from predators, making them almost invisible in their environment.

❖ **Why do animals need to hide from prey?**
Predators like the snow leopard use camouflage to sneak up on their prey. Their spotted fur helps them blend into the rocky terrain, making it easier to pounce!

❖ **How do predators use camouflage to hunt?**
Some predators, like the praying mantis, use camouflage to ambush their prey. They blend into plants or flowers, waiting for an unsuspecting insect to come too close.

❖ **Why do some animals mimic dangerous creatures?**
Animals like the mimic octopus or the hoverfly copy the appearance of dangerous creatures, like snakes or bees, to scare off predators without having to fight.

❖ **Do animals always use camouflage to hide?**
No! Sometimes animals use bright colors or patterns to warn predators that they are dangerous. For example, the poison dart frog has bright colors to signal that it's toxic. This kind of warning is called aposematism.

❖ **How do animals use camouflage in different environments?**
Animals like the polar bear have white fur to blend into snowy

environments, while desert animals like the sidewinder snake are sand-colored to disappear in the desert.

❖ **Why do some animals change their camouflage with the seasons?**
Animals like the arctic fox grow white fur in the winter to blend into the snow and brown fur in the summer to match the dirt and rocks, helping them hide year-round.

❖ **Can camouflage help with finding a mate?**
Yes! The male peacock uses its bright, flashy feathers to attract mates, while still blending into the forest when predators are near. Camouflage can sometimes help animals stand out to mates while hiding from danger.

❖ **Why do animals mimic the environment?**
Some animals, like the walking stick insect, look just like twigs or leaves so predators don't notice them. This kind of disguise keeps them safe without needing to run away.

❖ **Do birds use camouflage for their nests?**
Yes! Many birds, like the common nightjar, lay their eggs in nests that blend into the ground. Their speckled eggs and brown feathers make it hard for predators to find them.

❖ **Can camouflage help animals survive in extreme habitats?**
Yes! Animals living in extreme environments, like the snowshoe hare, rely heavily on their camouflage to avoid being eaten. In snowy areas, having white fur makes it much harder for predators to spot them.

❖ **Why do some animals pretend to be other animals?**
Some harmless animals, like the king snake, mimic the colors of dangerous animals like the venomous coral snake. This mimicry helps them avoid being attacked, as predators mistake them for the more dangerous species.

❖ **Do underwater creatures use camouflage?**
Absolutely! Fish like the flounder can change their skin color and pattern to match the sea floor, blending into the sand to avoid predators or sneak up on prey.

❖ **Can insects use camouflage to defend themselves?**
Yes! Insects like the moth often have wing patterns that look like tree bark or leaves, helping them stay hidden during the day when they are most vulnerable to predators.

❖ **What is disruptive coloration, and how do animals use it?**
Some animals, like zebras, use disruptive coloration—bold patterns like stripes—to confuse predators. When zebras move together in a herd, their stripes make it hard for predators to focus on one animal.

❖ **Do amphibians use camouflage too?**
Yes, amphibians like the wood frog use camouflage to blend into the forest floor. Their brown and green skin helps them avoid predators like snakes and birds.

❖ **Why do some animals mimic plants?**
Animals like the leaf insect mimic the shape and color of leaves to blend into their surroundings. This makes it difficult for predators to spot them when they are resting on plants.

❖ **Can camouflage help animals regulate their body temperature?**
Yes! The horned lizard can change its skin color to lighter shades in hot environments to reflect sunlight, keeping it cool while also blending into the sand.

❖ **Do animals use camouflage to protect their young?**
Yes! Many animals, like the sea turtle, lay their eggs in places where the color and texture of the sand or vegetation help hide them from predators.

❖ **Can predators use camouflage to confuse prey?**

Some predators, like the cheetah, have spots that help them blend into the tall grass. This makes it easier for them to get close to prey without being seen.

❖ **How do animals use camouflage to ambush prey?**

Predators like the trapdoor spider hide in burrows covered with soil or leaves. When an insect gets too close, the spider leaps out to capture its prey.

❖ **Do all animals that use camouflage have predators?**

No, even top predators like the snow leopard use camouflage. The snow leopard's spotted coat helps it blend into the rocky, snowy mountains where it hunts.

❖ **What's the most common reason animals use camouflage?**

The most common reason animals use camouflage is for protection from predators. Whether they are hiding in the trees, on the ground, or underwater, camouflage helps them stay safe.

❖ **How do predators overcome camouflage?**

Some predators, like the hawk, have excellent vision and can detect even the slightest movement. Even the best camouflage can be ineffective if an animal moves at the wrong time.

❖ This completes Chapter 3, filled with amazing facts about how animals use camouflage and mimicry to survive in the wild. These creatures are true masters of disguise, blending into their environments and fooling both prey and predators with their incredible tricks!

Fun Fact Quiz

What is the most common reason animals use camouflage?

A. To attract mates
B. To find food
C. To avoid predators
D. To regulate body temperature

Answer
C. To avoid predators

The most common reason animals use camouflage is for protection from predators. By blending into their surroundings, animals can hide from those who might want to eat them, whether they are in trees, on the ground, or underwater.

Record-Breaking Speedsters

Fastest Animals In The World

Get ready to be amazed as we dive into the world of speed! Animals across the globe have evolved to be incredibly fast, whether on land, in the air, or underwater. From the lightning-quick cheetah racing across the savanna to the astonishing peregrine falcon diving from the sky, these speedsters push the limits of what's possible. Let's discover just how fast these remarkable creatures can go!

❖ **Did you know that cheetahs can run up to 70 miles per hour?**
Cheetahs are the fastest land animals, sprinting at incredible speeds to catch their prey. They can accelerate faster than most sports cars, reaching 60 mph in just a few seconds!

❖ **Did you know the peregrine falcon is the fastest bird?**
When diving, the peregrine falcon can reach speeds of up to 240 miles per hour, making it the fastest animal on the planet. This incredible speed helps it catch birds mid-flight.

❖ **How fast can a sailfish swim?**
Sailfish are the fastest swimmers in the ocean, reaching speeds of 68 miles per hour. Their long, sleek bodies and sail-like dorsal fin help them glide through the water at breakneck speeds.

❖ **Did you know the black marlin is one of the fastest fish in the world?**
The black marlin can swim at speeds of up to 82 miles per hour. This fish is known for its powerful body and ability to leap out of the water in spectacular displays.

❖ **Can pronghorn antelope outrun most animals?**
Yes! Pronghorns can run at speeds of up to 55 miles per hour and maintain that speed for long distances. While they're not as fast as cheetahs, they have more stamina and can outrun most predators.

❖ **How fast can an ostrich run?**
Ostriches are the fastest birds on land, running at speeds of up to 45 miles per hour. Their long legs and powerful strides allow them to cover huge distances quickly.

❖ **Did you know dragonflies are the fastest flying insects?**
Dragonflies can reach speeds of up to 35 miles per hour, making them the fastest insects in the world. Their speed and agility help them catch prey mid-air with precision.

❖ **What makes greyhounds the fastest dog breed?**
Greyhounds are built for speed, running up to 45 miles per hour. Their slender bodies and long legs make them excellent sprinters in races.

❖ **Can the common swift stay in the air for a long time?**
Yes! The common swift holds the record for the longest continuous flight of any bird, spending up to 10 months in the air without landing. While it's not the fastest, it's incredibly impressive in terms of endurance!

❖ **Did you know the horsefly is the fastest biting insect?**
The horsefly can fly at speeds of up to 90 miles per hour, chasing down its prey with ease. These speedy insects are surprisingly quick for their size.

❖ **What's the fastest reptile?**
The spiny-tailed iguana holds the record for the fastest reptile, reaching speeds of 21 miles per hour. This lizard uses its speed to escape predators in the wild.

❖ **How fast can the golden eagle dive?**
The golden eagle is another bird of prey with impressive speed. When diving for food, it can reach speeds of up to 150 miles per hour.

❖ **Can kangaroos hop quickly?**

Yes! Kangaroos can hop at speeds of up to 35 miles per hour, using their powerful legs to cover great distances. Their large, muscular tails help them balance as they hop.

❖ **Did you know the fastest marine mammal is the common dolphin?**

The common dolphin can swim at speeds of up to 60 kilometers per hour (37 miles per hour), making it the fastest mammal in the ocean.

❖ **Can wolves run at high speeds?**

Yes! Wolves can run at speeds of up to 40 miles per hour when chasing prey. They use their speed and teamwork to bring down much larger animals.

❖ **How fast can a jackrabbit run?**

The jackrabbit is known for its incredible speed, reaching up to 45 miles per hour. Its powerful hind legs allow it to escape predators in a flash.

❖ **Did you know that the snow leopard is a fast predator?**

Snow leopards can reach speeds of 40 to 50 miles per hour when chasing prey in the mountains. They use their strong legs and flexible bodies to move swiftly on steep terrain.

❖ **How fast can a hare run?**

Hares are incredibly fast, sprinting at speeds of up to 45 miles per hour. Their long legs allow them to escape predators with ease.

Fun Fact Quiz

Which animal is the fastest land animal, capable of running up to 70 miles per hour?

A. Pronghorn Antelope
B. Cheetah
C. Greyhound
D. Snow Leopard

Answer
B. Cheetah

Cheetahs are the fastest land animals, capable of sprinting at speeds of up to 70 miles per hour to catch their prey. Their incredible acceleration allows them to reach 60 mph in just a few seconds!

Impressive Endurance

Now, let's explore the endurance champions of the animal kingdom! While some animals may be fast sprinters, others excel in long-distance journeys and survival against the odds. From the Arctic tern's epic migrations to the resilient camels traversing the desert, these incredible creatures showcase what it means to go the distance. Prepare to be inspired by their remarkable stamina and tenacity!

❖ **Did you know the Arctic tern travels more than 22,000 miles each year?**
The Arctic tern holds the record for the longest migration of any bird. It flies from the Arctic to Antarctica and back every year, covering thousands of miles without stopping.

❖ **Can camels go long distances without water?**
Yes! Camels can travel for days in the desert without needing water. Their bodies are built to conserve water and withstand harsh conditions, making them one of the most enduring animals.

❖ **Did you know that monarch butterflies migrate thousands of miles?**
Monarch butterflies make an extraordinary journey, traveling up to 3,000 miles each year from Canada to Mexico. This epic migration is one of the longest of any insect species.

❖ **What makes sea turtles endurance champions?**
Sea turtles swim thousands of miles during their migrations, often traveling across entire oceans to return to the same beaches where they were born to lay their eggs.

❖ **Did you know the wildebeest migration is one of the largest in the world?**
Every year, millions of wildebeests migrate across Africa's Serengeti, traveling more than 1,000 miles in search of fresh grasslands.

❖ **How far can a caribou travel?**

Caribou, also known as reindeer, migrate over 3,000 miles each year, making them one of the longest-distance land migrators.

❖ **Can emperor penguins withstand harsh cold?**

Yes! Emperor penguins trek across the frozen Antarctic for miles to reach their breeding grounds. They endure freezing temperatures and long distances in one of the most hostile environments on Earth.

❖ **Did you know the sperm whale can dive for over an hour?**

Sperm whales are endurance divers, holding their breath for up to 90 minutes while they hunt for food deep in the ocean.

❖ **How long can a horse run without stopping?**

Horses have incredible stamina and can run for miles without needing a break. In endurance races, some horses cover distances of over 100 miles in a single day.

❖ **Can dolphins swim long distances?**

Yes! Dolphins are known for their stamina, often swimming hundreds of miles over the course of a few days.

Fun Fact Quiz

Which animal migrates the longest distance each year, traveling more than 22,000 miles from the Arctic to Antarctica and back?

A. Monarch Butterfly
B. Arctic Tern
C. Caribou
D. Sea Turtle

Answer
B. Arctic Tern

The Arctic tern holds the record for the longest migration of any bird, flying over 22,000 miles each year in an incredible journey from the Arctic to Antarctica and back.

Surprising Speed Records

Finally, we'll uncover some of the most surprising speed records in the animal world! From the mantis shrimp's lightning-fast punch to the trap-jaw ant's rapid snap, these animals show that speed comes in all forms. Let's dive into these record-breaking wonders!

❖ **Did you know the mantis shrimp has the fastest punch in the animal kingdom?**
The mantis shrimp can punch its prey at speeds of up to 50 miles per hour, delivering a blow powerful enough to crack shells!

❖ **How fast can the trap-jaw ant snap its jaws?**
The trap-jaw ant's jaws can snap shut at speeds of 145 miles per hour, making them the fastest-moving jaws of any insect.

❖ **Can a flea jump faster than a blink of an eye?**
Yes! Fleas can jump with such force that their legs accelerate faster than a rocket. They can leap 200 times their body length in an instant.

❖ **Did you know a peregrine falcon's dive is faster than most cars?**
When hunting, the peregrine falcon dives at speeds of over 240 miles per hour, making it the fastest movement in the animal kingdom.

❖ **How fast can a chameleon shoot its tongue?**
Chameleons have tongues that can shoot out at speeds of 13 miles per hour to capture prey, like insects, in a split second.

❖ **What is the fastest snake strike?**
The death adder can strike at speeds of up to 100 milliseconds, making it one of the fastest striking snakes in the world.

❖ **Can a hummingbird beat its wings faster than any other bird?**
Yes! The ruby-throated hummingbird can beat its wings up to 80 times per second, allowing it to hover in place while feeding on nectar.

❖ **Did you know that some spiders can trap prey with incredible speed?**
Trapdoor spiders can leap out of their burrows at lightning speed to catch unsuspecting insects walking by.

❖ **How fast is the flick of a toad's tongue?**
Toads can flick their tongues at speeds of up to 4 meters per second, quickly snatching up insects.

This wraps up Chapter 4, packed with mind-blowing facts about some of the fastest and most enduring animals on Earth. These creatures are true speedsters, showing off their remarkable abilities to move quickly and far across land, sea, and air!

Fun Fact Quiz

What animal can punch its prey at speeds of up to 50 miles per hour, delivering a powerful blow capable of cracking shells?

A. Trap-jaw Ant
B. Mantis Shrimp
C. Peregrine Falcon
D. Death Adder

Answer
B. Mantis Shrimp

The mantis shrimp has the fastest punch in the animal kingdom, striking its prey at speeds of up to 50 miles per hour!

Animals with Superpowers

Regeneration And Healing

Have you ever wished you could grow back a lost body part? Some incredible animals can! In this section, we'll explore fascinating creatures that have the amazing ability to regenerate and heal. From axolotls to starfish, these animals showcase the incredible power of nature and survival.

❖ **Did you know that the axolotl can regrow entire limbs?**
Axolotls are famous for their ability to regenerate lost body parts, including limbs, spinal cords, hearts, and even parts of their brains! This amazing ability makes them one of nature's true superheroes.

❖ **How do starfish regenerate their arms?**
If a starfish loses an arm, it can regrow it over time. In some cases, a single arm can even regenerate an entirely new starfish if a part of the central disk is attached.

❖ **Did you know that certain lizards can regrow their tails?**
Many lizards, like geckos, can lose their tails when attacked by predators. After a while, they grow a new one, though the replacement tail is often shorter and less perfect than the original.

❖ **How do planarians regrow their entire bodies?**
Planarians, tiny flatworms, can regenerate their whole bodies from just a small piece of their tissue. If you cut one in half, both halves will grow into full worms!

❖ **Did you know that crabs can regenerate their claws?**
When crabs lose a claw in battle or to escape predators, they can regrow a new one. It takes several molts, but eventually, the new claw becomes just as strong as the original.

❖ **Can sea cucumbers regenerate their internal organs?**
Yes! When threatened, sea cucumbers can eject their internal

organs to distract predators. They later regenerate these organs in a process that takes several weeks.

❖ **Did you know that deer regrow their antlers every year?**
Male deer, or bucks, shed their antlers annually and grow new ones. The regrowth process is extremely fast, with antlers growing up to an inch per day!

❖ **How do salamanders heal their hearts?**
Salamanders are one of the few animals that can regenerate parts of their heart tissue after injury, helping them survive major heart damage.

❖ **Did you know that certain jellyfish can reverse aging?**
The immortal jellyfish (Turritopsis dohrnii) can revert back to its juvenile form after reaching adulthood, essentially reversing its aging process and potentially living forever.

❖ **How do flatworms regenerate after being cut in half?**
Flatworms are incredibly resilient and can regenerate their entire bodies if cut in half, thanks to their stem cells, which can form any type of tissue.

❖ **Can hydras regenerate their whole bodies?**
Yes! Hydras, small freshwater animals, can regenerate any part of their body, including their head, within just a few days. They don't age and can live indefinitely in the right conditions.

❖ **Did you know that earthworms can regenerate parts of their bodies?**
If an earthworm is cut in two, the head section can regrow a new tail, but the tail section cannot grow a new head. The regenerative abilities of earthworms depend on the species and the location of the injury.

❖ **Can flatworms form two new worms from one split?**

Yes! If you cut a flatworm in two, both halves can regenerate into two new worms. Each half will grow the necessary missing parts to become whole again.

❖ **How do newts regenerate their body parts?**

Newts can regrow almost any part of their body, including limbs, tails, and even their eyes! They are one of the most impressive regenerators in the animal kingdom.

❖ **Did you know that lobsters can regenerate their claws and legs?**

Lobsters can regrow lost claws, legs, and antennae. If a lobster loses a limb, it will eventually grow back, though it may take a few molts for the limb to reach its original size.

❖ **How do sea spiders regrow their legs?**

Sea spiders can regenerate their legs if they lose one. Young sea spiders regenerate faster than older ones, with the regrown limb becoming fully functional after a few molts.

❖ **Can frogs regenerate lost limbs?**

Frogs can regenerate lost limbs, but this ability decreases as they age. Young frogs have a much higher capacity for regeneration than adults.

❖ **Did you know that sharks can regenerate their teeth?**

Sharks continuously regrow teeth throughout their lives. When a tooth is lost, another one from the row behind it moves forward to take its place.

❖ **How do octopuses regenerate their arms?**

If an octopus loses an arm, it can regrow a new one. The new arm will have all the same capabilities as the original, including the ability to sense touch and manipulate objects.

❖ **Did you know sponges can regenerate from tiny fragments?**
Sponges can completely regenerate from small fragments of their bodies. If a sponge is broken apart, each piece can grow into a new sponge.

Fun Fact Quiz

What incredible ability do axolotls possess that makes them unique among animals?

A. They can regrow their limbs and organs
B. They can change color to blend in
C. They can fly short distances
D. They can breathe underwater like fish

Answer
A. They can regrow their limbs and organs

Axolotls are famous for their remarkable ability to regenerate lost body parts, including limbs, spinal cords, hearts, and even parts of their brains!

Night Vision And Super Senses

Imagine being able to see in the dark or hear sounds that are completely silent to us! Many animals possess extraordinary senses that help them navigate and survive in their environments. In this section, we'll uncover the remarkable abilities of creatures that can "see" in ways humans can only dream of.

❖ **Did you know that owls can see in almost total darkness?**
Owls have large eyes and more rods in their retinas, which help them see in the dark. Their eyes are specially adapted to capture even the faintest light, allowing them to hunt at night.

❖ **How do bats "see" in the dark?**
Bats use echolocation to navigate and hunt in complete darkness. By emitting high-pitched sounds and listening for the echoes, they can determine the size, shape, and distance of objects around them.

❖ **Did you know cats have night vision too?**
Cats' eyes have a special layer of cells called the tapetum lucidum, which reflects light back through the retina, allowing them to see in very low light. This gives them their characteristic glowing eyes in the dark.

❖ **How do pit vipers sense heat?**
Pit vipers, like rattlesnakes, have special heat-sensing pits on their faces that allow them to detect warm-blooded prey, even in complete darkness.

❖ **Did you know that certain fish can sense electric fields?**
Electric fish, like the electric eel, can generate electric fields and use them to sense their environment. This ability helps them navigate murky waters and hunt for prey.

❖ **How do moths find flowers at night?**
Moths have a heightened sense of smell, allowing them to detect flowers from great distances in the dark. Their antennae are covered in tiny sensors that pick up the scent of nectar.

❖ **Did you know that tarsiers have the largest eyes relative to body size?**
Tarsiers, small primates found in Southeast Asia, have enormous eyes that allow them to see in the dark. Each eye is about the size of their brain, making them exceptional night hunters.

❖ **How do sharks sense prey in murky waters?**
Sharks have special sensors called ampullae of Lorenzini, which detect electrical signals given off by the muscle movements of their prey, helping them hunt in dark, cloudy water.

❖ **Did you know that some birds can see ultraviolet light?**
Birds like kestrels can see ultraviolet light, which helps them track prey by following urine trails left by small animals like rodents.

❖ **How do dogs have such a strong sense of smell?**
Dogs have up to 300 million olfactory receptors in their noses, compared to humans' 6 million. This gives them an incredible ability to detect scents from great distances or trace faint odors.

❖ **Did you know that moles can "feel" their way through tunnels?**
Moles are nearly blind but have a highly sensitive sense of touch. Their noses and whiskers detect the slightest vibrations in the soil, helping them locate prey underground.

❖ **How do dolphins use echolocation?**
Dolphins emit high-pitched clicks and listen for the echoes to locate objects and prey in the water. This allows them to "see" their surroundings even in murky or deep water where light is scarce.

❖ **Can scorpions see in the dark?**

Scorpions have multiple pairs of eyes, and while they don't have the sharpest vision, they can see well in low light, allowing them to hunt at night.

❖ **Did you know that snakes can "smell" with their tongues?**

Snakes flick their tongues to collect scent particles from the air and ground, which are then analyzed by a special organ in their mouth called the Jacobson's organ.

❖ **How do polar bears navigate in the Arctic night?**

Polar bears have excellent night vision and a strong sense of smell, which helps them track seals through thick ice and snow even in the pitch-dark Arctic winter.

❖ **Did you know barn owls can hunt using only sound?**

Barn owls have such sensitive hearing that they can detect the slightest rustling of prey, like mice, even in total darkness. They can accurately pinpoint their location based solely on sound.

❖ **How do crickets "hear" through their legs?**

Crickets have special receptors on their legs that can detect sound vibrations. These help them navigate their environment and avoid predators, especially at night.

❖ **Did you know eagles have vision eight times sharper than humans?**

Eagles can spot prey from miles away thanks to their incredible eyesight. They have special fovea in their eyes that allow them to focus on small details, making them excellent hunters.

❖ **Can frogs hear underwater?**

Yes! Frogs have unique hearing abilities that allow them to detect both airborne and underwater sounds, which helps them locate mates and avoid predators in their wet environments.

❖ **How do elephants communicate through the ground?**

Elephants can "hear" low-frequency sounds and vibrations through their feet. This allows them to communicate with other elephants over long distances, even when they're out of sight.

Fun Fact Quiz

What unique ability do bats use to navigate in the dark?

A. Night vision
B. Echolocation
C. Infrared vision
D. Enhanced smell

Answer
B. Echolocation

Bats use echolocation to navigate and hunt in complete darkness. By emitting high-pitched sounds and listening for the echoes, they can determine the size, shape, and distance of objects around them.

Super Strength And Resilience

What if you could survive extreme temperatures or even the vacuum of space? Some animals have superpowers that allow them to endure the harshest conditions on Earth and beyond. In this section, we'll discover the incredible strength and resilience of animals that can thrive in the most challenging environments.

❖ **Did you know tardigrades can survive in space?**
Tardigrades, also known as water bears, can withstand extreme temperatures, radiation, and even the vacuum of space. They can survive without food or water for decades by going into a state called cryptobiosis.

❖ **How do ants carry objects many times their weight?**
Ants can carry objects up to 50 times their own body weight. Their muscles are much thicker in proportion to their bodies compared to larger animals, giving them incredible strength for their size.

❖ **Did you know that dung beetles are some of the strongest animals?**
Dung beetles can push balls of dung that weigh up to 1,141 times their own body weight. That's the equivalent of a human pushing a fully-loaded cement truck!

❖ **How do camels survive in extreme heat?**
Camels are built to survive in the harsh desert environment. They can go for weeks without water and have special adaptations that allow them to conserve water and withstand extreme heat.

❖ **Did you know polar bears have incredible stamina?**
Polar bears can swim for long distances, sometimes for days at a time, to reach land or ice. They've been known to swim over 60 miles without stopping in search of food.

❖ **How do cockroaches survive extreme conditions?**
Cockroaches are incredibly resilient. They can survive without food for up to a month, hold their breath for 40 minutes, and even withstand radiation levels far higher than most animals.

❖ **Did you know that orcas are one of the strongest predators in the ocean?**
Orcas, or killer whales, are apex predators with immense strength. They work together to hunt large prey, including seals, sharks, and even whales.

❖ **How do wood frogs survive being frozen?**
Wood frogs can freeze solid during the winter, with their hearts stopping and their bodies turning to ice. When the weather warms, they thaw out and continue their normal lives.

❖ **Did you know that albatrosses can fly for hours without flapping their wings?**
Albatrosses are endurance flyers, able to soar across oceans using wind currents. They can travel thousands of miles with very little effort, often flying for days without landing.

❖ **How do crocodiles survive months without eating?**
Crocodiles have slow metabolisms, allowing them to go months without food. They can survive long periods of time by conserving energy and living off the fat stored in their bodies.

❖ **Did you know that honey badgers are known for their toughness?**
Honey badgers have thick skin and a fearless attitude, allowing them to take on dangerous predators like lions and venomous snakes. They are nearly immune to snake venom and can recover from cobra bites!

❖ **How do sea turtles survive deep dives?**
Sea turtles can hold their breath for up to five hours while diving.

They slow their heart rate down to conserve oxygen, allowing them to stay submerged for long periods of time.

❖ Did you know that elephants are among the strongest land animals?

Elephants can lift objects weighing over 600 pounds with their trunks. They also use their strength to push down trees and carry heavy loads across vast distances.

❖ How do kangaroos use their legs for power?

Kangaroos have incredibly strong hind legs, allowing them to leap up to 30 feet in a single bound and travel long distances at high speeds to escape predators.

❖ Did you know that gorillas are incredibly strong?

Gorillas have immense upper body strength, capable of lifting up to 10 times their own body weight. They use their strength to defend themselves, build nests, and forage for food.

❖ How do penguins survive freezing temperatures?

Penguins have thick layers of blubber and tightly packed feathers that keep them warm in the freezing Antarctic environment. Emperor penguins huddle together in large groups to share body heat during the harsh winter.

❖ Did you know that mountain goats can climb nearly vertical cliffs?

Mountain goats have powerful legs and specialized hooves that allow them to scale steep, rocky surfaces. Their strength and agility help them escape predators and reach food in hard-to-reach places.

❖ How do arctic foxes survive in extreme cold?

Arctic foxes have thick fur and a compact body shape that helps them retain heat. They also have a high metabolism that allows them to stay active in freezing temperatures.

❖ **Did you know that blue whales are the largest and one of the strongest animals on Earth?**
Blue whales are the largest animals ever to live, weighing up to 200 tons. Despite their massive size, they can travel long distances and dive to incredible depths in search of food.

❖ **How do grizzly bears store energy for hibernation?**
Grizzly bears eat up to 90 pounds of food per day before hibernation to build up fat reserves. During hibernation, they survive solely on stored fat for several months, with their metabolism slowing down significantly.

As we've seen, the animal kingdom is full of incredible beings that possess extraordinary abilities. From regeneration and super senses to unmatched strength, these animals demonstrate the wonders of nature. Remember, there's so much more to discover about the amazing creatures that share our planet! Keep exploring, and who knows what other animal superpowers you might uncover!

Fun Fact Quiz

What animal can survive being frozen and then thaw out when the weather warms?

A. Polar bear
B. Wood frog
C. Tardigrade
D. Arctic fox

Answer
B. Wood frog

Wood frogs can freeze solid during the winter, with their hearts stopping and their bodies turning to ice. When the weather warms, they thaw out and continue their normal lives.

Unbelievable Animal Homes and Habitats

World's Strangest Nests And Burrows

In this section, we will explore the remarkable nests and burrows built by various animals. Each one serves a specific purpose, providing safety and comfort for their inhabitants. Get ready to learn about the ingenious ways these animal architects create their living spaces!

❖ **Did you know termites are master architects?**
Termite mounds can be over 30 feet tall! These complex structures are ventilated to keep the colony cool, with special chambers for nurseries, food storage, and even fungus farms.

❖ **Why do prairie dogs create underground cities?**
Prairie dogs live in extensive underground burrow systems called "towns." These tunnels can span miles and have multiple entrances and exits for safety, with separate rooms for nesting and sleeping.

❖ **Did you know that some birds use stones to make their nests?**
Male penguins gather the smoothest, most beautiful stones to create nests for their mates. These stone nests help elevate their eggs above the cold, wet ground, keeping them safe and warm.

❖ **How do beavers create dams and lodges?**
Beavers build dams to slow down rivers, creating calm ponds where they can construct their lodges. The lodges are made of sticks and mud and have underwater entrances to protect against predators.

❖ **Did you know meerkats share their homes with other animals?**
Meerkats dig large, intricate burrow systems where they live in family groups. They often share their burrows with animals like mongooses and ground squirrels, creating a bustling underground neighborhood.

ELI SPARK

❖ **Why do weaver birds create hanging nests?**
Weaver birds are known for their intricate, basket-like nests, which hang from tree branches. The male bird uses strips of grass to weave the nest, sometimes building several before the female chooses her favorite!

❖ **Did you know ants build their homes in towering structures?**
Leafcutter ants create enormous underground nests that can be as deep as 26 feet, with tunnels and chambers dedicated to growing fungi. These fungi are their primary food source, and they tend to their gardens with great care.

❖ **How do woodpeckers carve out their homes?**
Woodpeckers use their strong beaks to carve holes in tree trunks. These hollowed-out cavities become their nests, where they lay eggs and raise their young. The holes also provide insulation from the cold.

❖ **Did you know armadillos build burrows for safety?**
Armadillos dig burrows up to 15 feet long! They use their powerful claws to create underground tunnels, where they sleep and hide from predators.

❖ **How do moles navigate their underground labyrinths?**
Moles create long, winding tunnels underground to find food like worms and insects. Their sensitive noses help them navigate in the dark, and they can dig as much as 18 feet of tunnels in one hour!

❖ **Did you know that wombats dig burrows with backward-facing pouches?**
Wombats have strong legs and claws for digging extensive burrows. Their pouches face backward to prevent dirt from getting on their babies while they dig.

❖ **How do gophers build complex underground homes?**
Gophers dig long, winding tunnels with separate chambers for

sleeping, storing food, and even "bathrooms." They use their sharp teeth to move dirt and create escape routes in case of danger.

❖ Did you know certain spiders create silk nests?

Funnel web spiders build nests from silk in the shape of a funnel, often hidden in crevices. When prey walks over the web, the spider quickly grabs it from inside the funnel and pulls it into the nest.

❖ Why do puffins dig burrows on cliffs?

Puffins dig burrows into the sides of cliffs to protect their eggs from predators. These burrows can be as deep as 3 feet and are often located on remote, rocky coastlines.

❖ Did you know echidnas burrow to protect their young?

Echidnas, also known as spiny anteaters, dig burrows to keep their young safe. The female lays a single egg and carries it in a pouch until it hatches. Then, the baby echidna (called a puggle) stays in the burrow until it's strong enough to leave.

Fun Fact Quiz

Which animal is known for creating hanging nests from strips of grass?

A. Woodpecker
B. Weaver bird
C. Termite
D. Prairie dog

Answer
B. Weaver bird

Weaver birds are famous for their intricate, basket-like nests, which hang from tree branches. The male bird weaves the nest using strips of grass, sometimes building several before the female selects her favorite!

Underwater Homes

Now, let's plunge into the depths of the ocean to discover how marine animals construct their underwater homes. From the cozy dens of octopuses to vibrant coral reefs, the underwater world is filled with creativity and wonder. Join us as we unveil the incredible adaptations of these aquatic architects!

❖ **Did you know octopuses create cozy dens?**
Octopuses are master builders in the ocean. They collect rocks, shells, and even bottle caps to create a safe hiding place called a "den" where they sleep and hide from predators.

❖ **How do beavers create underwater homes?**
Beavers build their lodges in ponds, with entrances located underwater. This makes it hard for predators to reach them. Inside the lodge, they have dry chambers where they sleep, store food, and raise their young.

❖ **Did you know corals create entire underwater cities?**
Coral polyps build coral reefs, which are home to thousands of marine species. These reefs act like underwater cities, providing shelter and food for fish, crustaceans, and many other sea creatures.

❖ **Why do sea otters wrap themselves in kelp?**
Sea otters don't build permanent homes, but they use kelp forests as a safe resting spot. They wrap themselves in long strands of kelp to stay anchored and prevent drifting away while they sleep.

❖ **Did you know that clownfish live in sea anemones?**
Clownfish make their homes in the stinging tentacles of sea anemones. They are immune to the stings, and the anemone provides them with protection from predators while the clownfish helps keep the anemone clean.

❖ **How do crabs build homes out of shells?**
Hermit crabs use empty shells as their mobile homes. As they grow, they find bigger shells to move into, offering them both protection and mobility.

❖ **Did you know sponges are homes for tiny animals?**
Sea sponges, though they may seem simple, provide shelter for many tiny sea creatures like shrimp and small fish. The sponge's porous body offers hiding spots where these animals can live safely.

❖ **How do shrimps build burrows in the sea floor?**
Certain shrimp species, like the pistol shrimp, dig burrows in the sand on the sea floor. They use these burrows as both homes and traps to catch passing prey.

❖ **Did you know that fish can build nests?**
Some fish, like the stickleback, build nests on the riverbed using plants and algae. Male sticklebacks construct the nest and guard the eggs until they hatch.

❖ **How do starfish hide in the ocean?**
Starfish often hide under rocks or in crevices on the sea floor to avoid predators. Their flexible bodies allow them to squeeze into small spaces for safety.

❖ **Did you know that lobsters build tunnels in the sand?**
Lobsters create tunnels or burrows in the sand or mud at the bottom of the ocean. These tunnels serve as homes where they rest and protect themselves from predators.

❖ **How do sea turtles find their way back to the same beach?**
Sea turtles travel thousands of miles in the ocean but always return to the same beach where they were born to lay their eggs. They dig nests in the sand, where the eggs remain until they hatch.

❖ **Did you know squids live in caves?**

Certain squid species make their homes in underwater caves. These caves protect them from predators, and they use their ability to camouflage to blend into the rocky surroundings.

❖ **How do mussels create secure homes?**

Mussels attach themselves to rocks or other surfaces using strong, thread-like structures called byssal threads. These threads hold them securely in place, even in strong ocean currents.

❖ **Did you know that dolphins live in pods?**

Dolphins don't have physical homes, but they live in social groups called pods. These pods offer protection and support as the dolphins work together to hunt and raise their young.

Fun Fact Quiz

Which marine animal is known for living in a symbiotic relationship with sea anemones?

A. Octopus
B. Clownfish
C. Sea turtle
D. Hermit crab

Answer
B. Clownfish

Clownfish make their homes in the stinging tentacles of sea anemones. They are immune to the stings and receive protection from predators, while the clownfish helps keep the anemone clean!

Extreme Environments

In this part of the chapter, we will uncover how animals thrive in extreme environments. Whether in icy polar regions or scorching deserts, these resilient creatures have developed unique adaptations to survive. Prepare to be amazed by their extraordinary abilities to call some of the harshest habitats home!

❖ **Did you know polar bears create dens in the snow?**
Polar bears dig dens in snowdrifts to give birth and protect their cubs from the freezing Arctic weather. The dens are insulated by snow, keeping the inside much warmer than the outside.

❖ **How do camels survive in the desert?**
Camels can go days without water, and their humps store fat that provides energy when food is scarce. Their homes are the vast deserts, where they are well-adapted to the hot, dry conditions.

❖ **Did you know penguins build nests on ice?**
Emperor penguins build nests in the harsh Antarctic environment, often huddling together for warmth. They use rocks or simply gather in large groups to shield their eggs from the cold wind.

❖ **How do desert tortoises stay cool?**
Desert tortoises dig burrows to escape the intense heat of the desert. These underground homes provide shelter from both the sun and predators.

❖ **Did you know certain birds nest on the edges of cliffs?**
Birds like the northern fulmar nest on steep cliff faces, using these inaccessible locations to protect their eggs from predators.

❖ **How do mountain goats live in high altitudes?**
Mountain goats make their homes on rocky, steep slopes where few

predators can reach them. Their strong hooves allow them to climb nearly vertical cliffs to find food and stay safe.

❖ **Did you know that kangaroo rats survive without drinking water?**
Kangaroo rats, which live in deserts, get all the water they need from the seeds they eat. They build burrows in the sand to stay cool during the day.

❖ **How do Arctic foxes make homes in the tundra?**
Arctic foxes dig burrows in the frozen ground of the tundra.

As we wrap up this chapter on unbelievable animal homes and habitats, we've seen how diverse and creative the natural world can be. Animals have developed remarkable ways to construct their shelters, ensuring their survival in a variety of environments. Their ingenuity inspires us to appreciate the incredible adaptations that allow them to thrive in our world!

Fun Fact Quiz

Which animal can survive without drinking water by obtaining all the moisture it needs from its food?

A. Polar bear
B. Desert tortoise
C. Kangaroo rat
D. Mountain goat

Answer
C. Kangaroo rat

Kangaroo rats, which live in deserts, get all the water they need from the seeds they eat. They build burrows in the sand to stay cool during the day!

Animal Communication and Social Skills

How Animals Talk To Each Other

Did you know dolphins have names? In this section, we'll explore the various ways animals communicate, from using sounds and scents to body language. Let's dive into the incredible methods animals use to talk to one another!

❖ **Did you know dolphins have names?**
Dolphins use unique whistles to identify themselves, much like human names! Each dolphin has its own signature sound, which it uses to communicate with others in its pod.

❖ **How do bees tell each other where to find food?**
Bees perform a special "waggle dance" to show other bees the direction and distance of food sources. The dance is done in a figure-eight pattern, with the angle of the waggle indicating the direction of the food relative to the sun.

❖ **Did you know elephants communicate through the ground?**
Elephants send vibrations through the ground that can travel for miles. They use their feet to detect these vibrations, allowing them to "talk" with other elephants even when they're far away.

❖ **How do wolves communicate with their pack?**
Wolves use a combination of howls, body language, and scents to communicate. Their howls can signal location, mark territory, or call the pack together for a hunt.

❖ **Did you know birds sing to mark their territory?**
Many birds use song to let others know that a certain area belongs to them. The louder and more complex the song, the better the bird can defend its territory from rivals.

❖ **How do ants share information about food?**
Ants leave chemical trails, called pheromones, to guide other ants

to food sources. Once an ant finds food, it heads back to the nest, leaving a scent trail for others to follow.

❖ Did you know meerkats have different calls for different predators?

Meerkats use specific alarm calls depending on the type of predator. They have one call for eagles, another for snakes, and yet another for land predators like jackals.

❖ How do whales communicate across long distances?

Humpback whales sing complex songs that can travel hundreds of miles through the ocean. These songs help whales communicate with each other during migration or while hunting.

❖ Did you know that gorillas use chest-beating to communicate?

Gorillas beat their chests to display strength and dominance. This sound can be heard up to half a mile away and serves as a warning to other gorillas to stay out of their territory.

❖ How do fireflies "talk" with light?

Fireflies use light signals to communicate during courtship. Each species of firefly has a unique flash pattern, which helps males and females find each other.

❖ Did you know that cats communicate with humans through purring?

Cats purr for different reasons, including to express contentment, ask for food, or even heal themselves. The frequency of a cat's purr has been shown to promote healing and reduce stress.

❖ How do prairie dogs have their own "language"?

Prairie dogs have different vocalizations to describe specific predators. They can even convey information about the size, color, and speed of a predator, essentially creating their own detailed warning system.

❖ **Did you know that chimpanzees use gestures to communicate?**
Chimps have a repertoire of over 60 gestures to communicate with each other. They use these gestures to share food, request help, or even show affection.

❖ **How do peacocks use their feathers to talk?**
Male peacocks fan out their colorful feathers to attract females. The size and vibrancy of the tail display communicate strength and health to potential mates.

❖ **Did you know that crickets "sing" by rubbing their wings together?**
Male crickets create a chirping sound by rubbing their wings together to attract females. The faster the chirping, the more attractive they are to potential mates.

❖ **How do bats communicate with each other in the dark?**
Bats use echolocation, emitting high-pitched sounds that bounce off objects and return to them. This allows them to navigate and hunt in total darkness while also helping them "talk" to other bats.

❖ **Did you know that frogs call to attract mates?**
Male frogs croak to attract female frogs during the mating season. Each species has its own unique croak, which females listen for when choosing a mate.

❖ **How do penguins find each other in a crowded colony?**
Penguins use vocalizations to recognize their mates and chicks among thousands of other penguins. Even in large, noisy colonies, they can identify each other by the unique sound of their calls.

❖ **Did you know that hippos communicate underwater?**
Hippos make sounds both above and below water, using clicks and grunts to communicate with each other. They can even recognize their family members by the sound of their calls.

Fun Fact Quiz

What unique method do bees use to tell each other where to find food?

A. Dancing
B. Singing
C. Drumming
D. Whistling

Answer
A. Dancing

Bees perform a special "waggle dance" to show other bees the direction and distance of food sources! This incredible dance is done in a figure-eight pattern, helping other bees locate the food.

Teamwork In The Wild

Teamwork is essential for survival in the wild, and many animals have mastered the art of cooperation. In this section, we'll learn about communities of animals, like ants, bees, and wolves, that rely on each other to thrive. Prepare to be amazed by the power of teamwork in the animal world!

❖ **Did you know ants work together like a factory?**
In an ant colony, each ant has a specific role, such as gathering food, caring for the queen, or defending the nest. Their teamwork allows them to build complex nests and thrive as a community.

❖ **How do wolves hunt in packs?**
Wolves hunt as a team, with each member of the pack playing a role in bringing down prey. They communicate through howls and body language to coordinate their movements during the hunt.

❖ **Did you know meerkats take turns standing guard?**
In a meerkat group, one or two members will always act as lookouts while the rest of the group forages. The guards keep watch for predators and alert the group with warning calls if danger is near.

❖ **How do dolphins work together to catch fish?**
Dolphins often hunt in groups, using teamwork to herd schools of fish into tight balls, making them easier to catch. They communicate with each other using clicks and whistles to coordinate their movements.

❖ **Did you know honeybees have specialized jobs?**
In a hive, worker bees are responsible for gathering nectar, building honeycombs, and taking care of the queen. Each bee has a specific task, and together they create a thriving colony.

❖ **How do lions share the task of raising cubs?**
In a lion pride, females work together to care for the cubs, often nursing each other's young. This cooperation helps ensure the survival of the entire pride.

❖ **Did you know that elephants show teamwork when caring for their young?**
In an elephant herd, older females help care for the babies, teaching them how to find food and water. This cooperative parenting helps ensure the calves grow up strong and safe.

❖ **How do penguins survive the cold by huddling together?**
Emperor penguins huddle together in large groups to stay warm during the harsh Antarctic winter. They take turns standing on the outside of the huddle, where it's coldest, and then rotate to the warmer center.

❖ **Did you know that fish schools swim in perfect synchrony?**
Fish in schools swim together in coordinated patterns to confuse predators. By moving as one, they make it harder for a predator to target a single fish.

❖ **How do crows work together to solve problems?**
Crows are incredibly intelligent and often work together to find food or solve puzzles. They've been known to use tools and even work in teams to open containers or steal food from other animals.

❖ **Did you know that chimpanzees share food with each other?**
In chimpanzee groups, individuals often share food with one another, particularly after a successful hunt. This sharing helps strengthen social bonds within the group.

❖ **How do termites build such massive structures?**
Termites work together to build towering mounds that can be over 30 feet tall. Each termite has a specific job, and their teamwork

results in impressive, ventilated homes that can house millions of individuals.

❖ **Did you know orcas work together to catch prey?**
Orcas, also known as killer whales, hunt in pods, using teamwork to corner and catch prey like fish or seals. They communicate through clicks and whistles to strategize during a hunt.

❖ **How do buffalo protect each other from predators?**
When faced with danger, buffalo herds form a circle with the young in the center and the strongest adults on the outside. This teamwork protects the vulnerable members of the herd from predators.

Fun Fact Quiz

How do dolphins work together to catch fish?

A. They swim in circles
B. They create a loud noise
C. They herd fish into tight balls
D. They dive underwater

Answer
C. They herd fish into tight balls

Dolphins often hunt in groups, using teamwork to herd schools of fish into tight balls, making it easier for them to catch their food. This coordinated effort showcases the power of collaboration in the animal kingdom!

Unique Mating Rituals

When it comes to courtship, some animals go all out! From birds performing dazzling dances to frogs singing songs, we'll discover some of the most unique and entertaining mating rituals in the animal kingdom. Get ready for some incredible love stories!

❖ **Did you know birds of paradise put on an elaborate dance for their mates?**
Male birds of paradise perform intricate dances, displaying their colorful feathers to impress females. Some of their moves are so complex they look like they're straight out of a dance competition!

❖ **How do peacocks attract a mate with their stunning tail feathers?**
Male peacocks fan out their brilliant tail feathers in an impressive display to attract females. The size and color of the tail feathers are key factors in attracting a mate.

❖ **Did you know that seahorses dance for days before mating?**
Seahorses engage in a courtship dance that can last for days! They intertwine their tails and mirror each other's movements as they float through the water.

❖ **How do flamingos synchronize their movements during courtship?**
During mating season, flamingos perform a synchronized dance, moving together in a large group. This coordinated movement helps them attract mates and strengthen social bonds.

❖ **Did you know that penguins present rocks to their mates?**
Male penguins collect the smoothest, most perfect pebbles to offer to females as part of their courtship. If the female accepts the rock, they begin building a nest together.

❖ **How do bowerbirds build elaborate structures to impress mates?**

Male bowerbirds create intricate structures, called bowers, using sticks, leaves, and brightly colored objects. They decorate these bowers with berries, shells, and flowers to impress females.

❖ **Did you know that frogs sing to attract mates?**

Male frogs croak loudly to attract female frogs during the mating season. The louder the croak, the more likely they are to find a mate.

❖ **How do spiders use vibrations to court mates?**

Male spiders create vibrations in the web to communicate with potential mates. The vibrations signal that they're interested in mating and help avoid being mistaken for prey.

❖ **Did you know that fireflies flash lights to find a partner?**

Male fireflies use a series of flashes to attract females. Each species has its own unique light pattern, making it easier for them to find the right mate.

❖ **How do emperor penguins find their lifelong partners?**

Emperor penguins are known to mate for life. They perform a special courtship ritual involving head-bowing and vocalizing to strengthen their bond with their mate.

As we conclude this chapter on animal communication and social skills, we've uncovered how animals connect, cooperate, and communicate in truly remarkable ways. Their social interactions not only help them survive but also make the animal world endlessly fascinating!

Fun Fact Quiz

How do flamingos synchronize their movements during courtship?

A. They dance individually
B. They perform a synchronized dance
C. They sing together
D. They fly in formation

Answer
B. They perform a synchronized dance

During mating season, flamingos perform a synchronized dance, moving together in a large group. This coordination helps them attract mates and strengthen social bonds, showcasing the beauty of teamwork in their courtship rituals!

Weird and Wonderful
Animal Adaptations

Extreme Adaptations For Survival

Some animals have evolved with unbelievable traits to help them survive. Whether it's the venomous bite of a komodo dragon or the gliding ability of a flying squirrel, these creatures are masters of adaptation. Let's explore the extreme abilities animals use to stay alive!

❖ **Did you know the komodo dragon has venomous saliva?**
The bite of a komodo dragon delivers venom that can cause shock and blood loss, helping them overpower prey. Their saliva contains bacteria that makes the wound even more deadly.

❖ **How do flying squirrels glide through the air?**
Flying squirrels have a special membrane between their legs called the patagium, which they use to glide between trees. They can cover distances of up to 150 feet in a single glide!

❖ **Did you know that the archerfish can shoot water at its prey?**
Archerfish can accurately spit water to knock insects off branches and into the water. Their aim is so precise, they can hit a target from several feet away.

❖ **How do cuttlefish change color to blend in?**
Cuttlefish have specialized skin cells called chromatophores that allow them to change color and texture. This helps them camouflage with their surroundings or communicate with other cuttlefish.

❖ **Did you know that a horned lizard can shoot blood from its eyes?**
When threatened, horned lizards can squirt blood from their eyes to startle predators. This blood also has a foul taste, which deters predators from continuing their attack.

❖ **How do octopuses escape predators using ink?**
Octopuses can squirt a cloud of ink to create a smokescreen, allowing them to escape predators. The ink confuses their enemies and gives the octopus time to swim away.

❖ **Did you know kangaroo rats can live without drinking water?**
Kangaroo rats get all the moisture they need from the seeds they eat, allowing them to survive in desert environments without ever drinking water.

❖ **How do sea cucumbers defend themselves by ejecting their insides?**
When threatened, sea cucumbers can expel their internal organs to distract predators. They can later regenerate the lost organs, continuing their life cycle as if nothing happened.

❖ **Did you know that tardigrades can survive in space?**
Tardigrades, also known as water bears, can survive extreme conditions like freezing temperatures, radiation, and even the vacuum of space. They enter a dormant state called cryptobiosis to withstand harsh environments.

❖ **How do wood frogs freeze solid in winter and come back to life?**
Wood frogs have the incredible ability to freeze during winter and then thaw out in spring without any harm. They produce a natural antifreeze that protects their cells from damage during freezing.

❖ **Did you know that platypuses have electroreception?**
The platypus can detect the electric fields produced by the movements of other animals. This allows them to hunt underwater, even in murky or dark conditions.

❖ **How do penguins survive freezing temperatures in Antarctica?**
Penguins have a thick layer of fat and densely packed feathers that

keep them insulated in freezing temperatures. They also huddle together in large groups to conserve warmth.

❖ Did you know the basilisk lizard can run on water?

The basilisk lizard, also known as the "Jesus lizard," can run across the surface of water using its long toes to spread its weight. This helps it escape from predators quickly.

❖ How do camels survive in the desert with minimal water?

Camels can store fat in their humps, which they use as energy when food and water are scarce. They can also go for long periods without drinking by conserving water in their bodies.

❖ Did you know that star-nosed moles have super-sensitive noses?

The star-nosed mole has a unique, star-shaped nose with 22 tiny appendages that are incredibly sensitive. It uses this nose to detect and identify prey in total darkness.

❖ How do monarch butterflies navigate thousands of miles during migration?

Monarch butterflies use the sun and Earth's magnetic field to guide them during their long migrations. They travel over 2,500 miles from North America to Central Mexico each year.

❖ Did you know that the mimic octopus can imitate other animals?

The mimic octopus can change its appearance to look like other sea creatures, such as lionfish or sea snakes. This helps it avoid predators by pretending to be more dangerous animals.

❖ How do polar bears stay warm in the Arctic?

Polar bears have thick fur and a layer of blubber to keep them insulated in the freezing Arctic temperatures. Their fur even appears white to blend in with the snow, but it is actually transparent!

❖ **Did you know that armadillos can roll into a ball for protection?**
Armadillos can curl into a tight ball, using their armored shell as protection from predators. This makes it nearly impossible for predators to reach their soft undersides.

❖ **How do electric eels generate electricity?**
Electric eels have specialized cells called electrocytes that can produce powerful electric shocks, which they use to stun prey or defend themselves from predators.

Fun Fact Quiz

How do electric eels generate electricity?

A. By using their muscles
B. Through specialized cells called electrocytes
C. By breathing underwater
D. By swimming quickly

Answer
B. Through specialized cells called electrocytes

Electric eels have specialized cells called electrocytes that can produce powerful electric shocks. They use these shocks to stun prey or defend themselves from predators, showcasing their incredible adaptations for survival!

Animals That Glow

Imagine glowing in the dark! Some animals can do just that, using bioluminescence to light up their surroundings. From jellyfish to fireflies, we'll discover how glowing helps animals navigate, communicate, and avoid predators.

❖ **Did you know fireflies use their light to attract mates?**
Fireflies produce light through a chemical reaction called bioluminescence. The flashing patterns help males and females find each other in the dark during mating season.

❖ **How do deep-sea anglerfish lure prey with their glowing "fishing rod"?**
Female anglerfish have a glowing lure that dangles in front of their mouths. This light attracts smaller fish, which the anglerfish then devours when they come close.

❖ **Did you know that certain species of jellyfish glow in the dark?**
Jellyfish can produce light through bioluminescence, which helps them deter predators or attract prey in the deep ocean where sunlight doesn't reach.

❖ **How do glowworms light up caves?**
Glowworms produce a soft blue light that attracts insects into their sticky silk threads. These glowing traps help them catch food in the dark.

❖ **Did you know that the vampire squid uses glowing displays to escape predators?**
The vampire squid can release a cloud of glowing mucus to confuse predators and make a quick escape in the dark ocean depths.

❖ **How do certain types of fungi glow in the dark?**
Some species of fungi, like the "foxfire" mushrooms, emit a faint greenish light. This bioluminescence may help attract insects that assist in spreading their spores.

❖ **Did you know that scorpions glow under ultraviolet light?**
Scorpions have a natural glow when exposed to UV light. Scientists aren't sure why, but it could help them detect each other or protect them from sunlight.

❖ **How do plankton create glowing waves?**
Bioluminescent plankton produce a glowing blue light when disturbed by waves or movement in the water. This can create an otherworldly glow in the ocean at night.

❖ **Did you know that certain species of squid light up to communicate?**
Some squid can control their bioluminescence to send signals to other squid or to confuse predators by creating dazzling light displays.

❖ **How do lanternfish use their glow to hide in the deep sea?**
Lanternfish produce light on their undersides to match the faint light from above, helping them avoid being seen by predators lurking below.

❖ **Did you know that firefly squid can produce different colors of light?**
The firefly squid can emit flashes of blue, green, and white light. This helps them communicate with other squid or attract prey in the dark depths of the ocean.

❖ **How do glowing corals survive in the ocean?**
Some corals glow under UV light due to proteins in their tissues. This glow may help protect them from harmful sunlight or attract prey.

❖ **Did you know that flashlight fish use light to hunt?**

Flashlight fish have glowing patches under their eyes that they use to hunt in the dark. They can control when the light is visible, helping them find food while staying hidden from predators.

❖ **How do certain species of sea stars glow to escape predators?**

Some sea stars can produce a glowing light when disturbed, which helps them distract predators and make an escape in the dark ocean.

Fun Fact Quiz

How do certain species of sea stars glow to escape predators?

A. By changing color
B. By releasing ink
C. By producing a glowing light when disturbed
D. By swimming quickly

Answer
C. By producing a glowing light when disturbed

Some sea stars can produce a glowing light when disturbed. This bioluminescence helps distract predators, allowing the sea stars to make a quick escape in the dark ocean!

Cold-Blooded Wonders

Cold-blooded animals like reptiles and amphibians have amazing ways to adapt to their environments. From slowing down their metabolism to changing their body temperature, these creatures have mastered survival in some of the world's harshest conditions. Let's take a look at how they do it!

❖ **Did you know that snakes can go months without eating?**
Snakes, like other cold-blooded animals, have slower metabolisms, allowing them to survive long periods without food. They can wait for the perfect opportunity to strike their prey.

❖ **How do crocodiles stay warm by basking in the sun?**
Crocodiles spend hours basking in the sun to raise their body temperature. As cold-blooded animals, they rely on the sun to stay warm and active.

❖ **Did you know that some lizards can change color to regulate their temperature?**
Lizards, like the chameleon, can adjust their color to absorb more heat from the sun or reflect light to stay cool. This helps them manage their body temperature throughout the day.

❖ **How do frogs survive freezing winters by going dormant?**
Some frogs enter a state of dormancy, or hibernation, during cold weather. Their bodies slow down, and they can even freeze partially, only to thaw out and wake up in spring.

❖ **Did you know that iguanas can "play dead" to escape predators?**
When threatened, iguanas can remain motionless and blend into their surroundings, making them appear lifeless to predators. This behavior helps them avoid detection.

❖ **How do tortoises survive in hot, dry environments?**

Tortoises can dig burrows to escape the intense heat of the desert. They can also store water in their bodies, allowing them to survive for long periods without drinking.

❖ **Did you know that alligators can "sleep" underwater for hours?**

Alligators can lower their heart rate and hold their breath for extended periods. This allows them to rest underwater or stay hidden from prey and predators.

❖ **How do salamanders regenerate lost limbs?**

Salamanders can regrow lost limbs, including tails and even parts of their heart or spinal cord. This remarkable ability helps them survive injuries in the wild.

❖ **Did you know that cold-blooded animals rely on the environment to stay active?**

Unlike warm-blooded animals, cold-blooded creatures need external heat sources like the sun to maintain their energy levels. If it's too cold, they become sluggish.

❖ **How do komodo dragons use their slow metabolism to their advantage?**

Komodo dragons can go weeks between meals due to their slow metabolism. This allows them to survive in environments where food is scarce.

As we wrap up this chapter, we've seen how animals use their weird and wonderful adaptations to survive and thrive in diverse environments. These unique traits remind us of the incredible diversity of life on Earth, each creature perfectly suited to its way of living!

Fun Fact Quiz

How do komodo dragons use their slow metabolism to their advantage?

A. By eating constantly
B. By going weeks between meals
C. By being active all the time
D. By sleeping a lot

Answer
B. By going weeks between meals

Komodo dragons have a slow metabolism that allows them to go weeks without eating, helping them survive in environments where food is scarce!

Fascinating Animal
Life Cycles

Strange And Unique Births

Some animals bring their babies into the world in the most surprising ways. From kangaroos carrying their young in pouches to seahorse dads giving birth, get ready to uncover the weirdest and most wonderful birth stories in the animal kingdom!

❖ **Did you know male seahorses are the ones who give birth?**
In seahorse species, it's the males who carry the eggs in a special pouch. After several weeks, the male gives birth to dozens, or even hundreds, of tiny seahorses.

❖ **How do kangaroos care for their babies in their pouches?**
Kangaroo babies, called joeys, are born tiny and undeveloped. They crawl into their mother's pouch where they continue to grow and develop, staying there for up to six months.

❖ **Did you know some frogs give birth through their skin?**
The Surinam toad lays eggs that embed themselves in the female's back. When the tadpoles are ready, they hatch right out of the mother's skin!

❖ **How do monotremes like the platypus lay eggs instead of giving live birth?**
Unlike most mammals, monotremes such as the platypus and echidna lay eggs. After hatching, the mother feeds her young with milk, but she doesn't **have nipples, so the milk oozes through her skin.**

❖ **Did you know that certain sharks give birth to live young?**
Some shark species, like the great white shark, have live births. The babies, called pups, are fully developed when they are born and can swim away immediately to survive on their own.

ELI SPARK

❖ **How do marsupial moles give birth in underground tunnels?**
Marsupial moles are born in shallow tunnels dug by their mothers. The babies latch onto their mother's milk until they are strong enough to burrow on their own.

❖ **Did you know that giraffes give birth standing up?**
When a giraffe gives birth, the baby falls about six feet to the ground! This fall helps break the amniotic sac and kick-starts the baby's breathing.

❖ **How do emperor scorpions carry their babies on their backs?**
After giving birth, female emperor scorpions carry their newborns on their backs until they are ready to fend for themselves. The babies cling to their mother's body for protection and nourishment.

❖ **Did you know that the male pipefish also carries and gives birth to offspring?**
Similar to seahorses, male pipefish carry fertilized eggs in a specialized pouch until they hatch. The male then releases the young into the water when they are fully developed.

❖ **How do armadillos give birth to identical quadruplets?**
Armadillos always give birth to identical quadruplets. Each litter comes from a single fertilized egg that splits into four embryos, resulting in four genetically identical offspring.

❖ **Did you know that elephant pregnancies last nearly two years?**
Elephants have the longest gestation period of any land animal, with pregnancies lasting around 22 months! This long development time ensures the calf is strong and healthy when born.

❖ **How do flamingos lay their eggs on mud nests?**
Flamingos build tall, cone-shaped nests out of mud to keep their

eggs safe from flooding. The parents take turns incubating the egg until it hatches.

❖ Did you know that the kiwi bird lays an enormous egg?

The kiwi bird lays an egg that can weigh up to a quarter of its own body weight! After laying this massive egg, the male kiwi incubates it for about 80 days until it hatches.

❖ How do surinam cockroaches give birth to live nymphs?

Unlike most insects that lay eggs, surinam cockroaches give birth to live young. The babies are fully developed when they emerge, ready to fend for themselves.

❖ Did you know some snakes give birth to live young?

While many snakes lay eggs, some species, like the boa constrictor, give birth to live babies. These young snakes are independent from birth and can hunt on their own immediately.

❖ How do marsupial sugar gliders raise their babies in tree hollows?

Sugar gliders give birth to tiny, underdeveloped babies that crawl into their mother's pouch, where they continue to develop. Once they are ready, the mother raises them in tree hollows.

❖ Did you know octopuses lay thousands of eggs at once?

Female octopuses lay up to 200,000 eggs, which they carefully guard and oxygenate by blowing water over them. The mother stays with her eggs until they hatch, often dying soon after.

❖ How do penguins protect their eggs from the cold?

Male emperor penguins incubate the egg by balancing it on their feet and covering it with a flap of skin called a brood pouch. They protect the egg through harsh Antarctic winters, waiting for it to hatch.

❖ **Did you know that some amphibians carry their eggs in special sacs?**
Some frogs and salamanders carry fertilized eggs in specialized pouches on their bodies. These sacs protect the eggs and keep them moist until they hatch.

❖ **How do seahorse babies survive without parental care after birth?**
Seahorse fathers give birth to hundreds of tiny babies, but once they're born, they receive no further care. The babies must fend for themselves from the moment they are released into the ocean.

Fun Fact Quiz

Did you know male seahorses are the ones who give birth?

A. Yes, they carry eggs in a pouch
B. No, females are responsible for birth
C. Only in some species
D. They do not give birth

Answer
A. Yes, they carry eggs in a pouch

In seahorse species, the males carry the eggs in a special pouch and give birth to dozens or even hundreds of tiny seahorses after several weeks!

Metamorphosis Masters

Metamorphosis is one of nature's most dramatic changes. Whether it's a caterpillar becoming a butterfly or a tadpole growing into a frog, we'll take a close look at animals that undergo incredible transformations throughout their lives.

❖ **Did you know that caterpillars completely transform into butterflies?**
Caterpillars go through metamorphosis inside a chrysalis, where their entire body changes into a butterfly. This process can take a few weeks, but the result is an entirely new creature!

❖ **How do tadpoles become frogs?**
Tadpoles start their life in water with gills and a tail, but as they grow, they develop lungs and legs, eventually turning into adult frogs that can live both in water and on land.

❖ **Did you know that dragonflies begin their life underwater?**
Dragonfly larvae, called nymphs, spend up to five years living underwater before they transform into adult dragonflies. Once they emerge, they only live for a few months as they focus on reproduction.

❖ **How do ladybugs go through four stages of life?**
Ladybugs start as eggs, hatch into larvae, then pupate into adults. Each stage looks completely different, with the adult ladybug being the final form, known for its bright red shell with black spots.

❖ **Did you know that butterflies and moths are born as caterpillars?**
Butterflies and moths start as tiny eggs, hatch into caterpillars, and then enter a pupal stage before emerging as winged adults. This complete metamorphosis allows them to experience two distinct lifestyles.

❖ **How do beetles transform from larvae into adults?**
Many beetles start their life as grubs, eating and growing before pupating. After their transformation, they emerge as adult beetles with hard exoskeletons and wings.

❖ **Did you know that cicadas spend years underground before emerging?**
Cicada nymphs live underground for several years, feeding on plant roots. When they are ready, they emerge from the soil, shed their exoskeletons, and become flying adults.

❖ **How do crabs go through multiple stages in their life cycle?**
Crabs start as tiny larvae that float in the ocean. As they grow, they molt their shells several times, eventually becoming adult crabs that live on the seafloor.

❖ **Did you know that starfish can regenerate their arms?**
If a starfish loses an arm, it can grow a new one! Some species can even regrow their entire body from just one arm. This ability helps them survive attacks from predators.

❖ **How do mosquitoes go through metamorphosis in water?**
Mosquitoes start their life as eggs laid on water. The larvae hatch and live in the water until they pupate and emerge as adult mosquitoes, ready to fly and search for food.

❖ **Did you know that frogs can change color during metamorphosis?**
Some species of frogs undergo color changes as they transition from tadpoles to adults. These color adaptations help them blend into their new environments as they move from water to land.

❖ **How do ants go through four stages of life?**
Ants start as eggs, hatch into larvae, and then enter the pupal stage before becoming adults. Each stage has its own role in the colony, from worker ants to queens.

❖ **Did you know that crickets molt several times before becoming adults?**
Crickets go through multiple molting stages as they grow, shedding their exoskeletons each time. After several molts, they reach their adult form and develop wings.

❖ **How do frogs breathe through their skin during metamorphosis?**
As tadpoles, frogs use gills to breathe underwater. As they transition to adulthood, they develop lungs but can also absorb oxygen through their skin in water or on land.

❖ **Did you know that jellyfish have a two-part life cycle?**
Jellyfish start as tiny polyps attached to the ocean floor. These polyps eventually bud off into free-swimming medusas, which is the adult form of a jellyfish.

❖ **How do newts regenerate lost limbs during metamorphosis?**
Newts can regrow lost limbs, including tails and even parts of their heart. This regeneration ability is particularly strong during their larval stages as they transform into adults.

❖ **Did you know that moths use silk cocoons for protection during metamorphosis?**
Moth larvae, also known as caterpillars, spin silk cocoons to protect themselves during their pupal stage. Inside the cocoon, they undergo **metamorphosis and emerge as adult moths.**

❖ **How do axolotls remain in their larval form throughout their life?**
Unlike most amphibians, axolotls retain their gills and stay in the water their entire life, even as adults. This unique adaptation allows them to stay in a larval state while still reproducing.

❖ **Did you know that termites undergo incomplete metamorphosis?**

Termites hatch from eggs and go through a series of molts as they grow. They don't undergo a pupal stage like other insects, but instead, transition directly into their adult form.

❖ **How do spiders go through a simple life cycle?**

Spiders hatch from eggs, molt several times as they grow, and eventually become adults. Unlike insects, they don't have a larval or pupal stage, making their life cycle simpler.

Fun Fact Quiz

Did you know that caterpillars completely transform into butterflies?

A. Yes, they go through metamorphosis
B. No, they stay the same
C. Only some caterpillars do
D. They don't transform at all

Answer
A. Yes, they go through metamorphosis

Caterpillars undergo a complete metamorphosis inside a chrysalis, changing into a butterfly over a few weeks. This fascinating transformation results in an entirely new creature!

Longevity And Short Lifespans

From creatures that live for just a day to those that can survive for centuries, the lifespans of animals are truly astounding. In this section, we'll discover which animals hold the records for the longest and shortest lives on Earth!

❖ **Did you know the mayfly lives for just one day?**
Mayflies have one of the shortest lifespans in the animal kingdom. After spending up to a year as aquatic larvae, they emerge as adults only to mate and die within 24 hours.

❖ **How do Greenland sharks live for hundreds of years?**
Greenland sharks have the longest lifespan of any vertebrate, with some individuals estimated to be over 500 years old! Their slow growth and deep-sea habitat contribute to their extreme longevity.

❖ **Did you know the queen termite can live up to 50 years?**
While most termites only live for a few years, a queen termite can live for decades, continuously laying thousands of eggs during her lifetime.

❖ **How do giant tortoises live to be over 100 years old?**
Galápagos and Aldabra giant tortoises can live well over a century, with some individuals reaching 150 years or more. Their slow metabolism and protected island habitats help them live long lives.

❖ **Did you know the ocean quahog clam can live for more than 500 years?**
The ocean quahog clam holds the record for the longest-lived animal, with one clam found to be over 500 years old. They grow extremely slowly, which is a key factor in their incredible longevity.

❖ **How do fruit flies complete their entire life cycle in just a few weeks?**

Fruit flies have one of the shortest lifespans of any insect. From egg to adult, their life cycle lasts only about 30 days, making them popular for scientific research.

❖ Did you know the bowhead whale can live for over 200 years?
Bowhead whales are among the longest-living mammals, with some individuals living over two centuries. They are slow swimmers, which might contribute to their long lifespan.

❖ How do houseflies live for just a few weeks?
A typical housefly only lives for around 28 days. During this short time, they go through four stages: egg, larva, pupa, and adult, quickly **completing their life cycle.**

❖ Did you know that lobsters might live forever if not caught?
Lobsters don't seem to age in the traditional sense and continue growing throughout their lives. Some scientists believe they could theoretically live indefinitely if they avoid predators and disease.

❖ How do elephants live for up to 70 years?
Elephants are the longest-living land animals, with lifespans that can reach 70 years or more. Their social structure and intelligence contribute to their long lives.

❖ Did you know that the immortal jellyfish can technically live forever?
The "immortal" jellyfish (Turritopsis dohrnii) can revert its cells to an earlier stage of life, essentially restarting its life cycle. This allows it to escape aging and, potentially, live indefinitely.

❖ How do the short-lived mayflies maximize their time?
Despite living for only 24 hours as adults, mayflies use their short lives to mate and lay eggs. Their entire existence is centered on reproduction, **ensuring the next generation is born.**

❖ **Did you know that parrots can live for over 80 years?**

Some species of parrots, like the macaw, have remarkably long lifespans and can live to be 80 years old or more. This makes them lifelong companions for their human caregivers.

❖ **How do dogs vary greatly in lifespan depending on their breed?**

Smaller dog breeds, like Chihuahuas, can live up to 20 years, while larger breeds, like Great Danes, often live only 7 to 10 years. Size is a major factor in determining their lifespans.

❖ **Did you know that some bats live up to 40 years?**

Despite their small size, some bat species, like the Brandt's bat, can live for over 40 years, making them one of the longest-living small mammals.

❖ **How do naked mole rats live 10 times longer than other rodents?**

Naked mole rats have a lifespan of up to 30 years, which is remarkable for a rodent. Their unique social structure and resistance to cancer contribute to their extended lifespan.

❖ **Did you know that goldfish can live for over 40 years?**

When cared for properly, goldfish can live for several decades. Some pet goldfish have been known to live up to 40 years, far outliving most expectations.

❖ **How do the albatrosses' long lives help them succeed?**

Albatrosses are among the longest-living birds, with lifespans of 50 years or more. Their long life allows them to travel vast distances and successfully raise multiple generations of chicks.

❖ **Did you know that spiders like tarantulas can live for over 30 years?**

Female tarantulas often live much longer than males, with some surviving up to 30 years or more. Their solitary lifestyle and efficient hunting techniques contribute to their longevity.

❖ **How do hummingbirds have such short lifespans despite their speed?**
Hummingbirds, known for their rapid wing beats, typically live for 3 to 5 years, though some individuals can live up to 9 years. Their fast metabolism and constant need for food shorten their lifespan.

These fascinating facts about animal life cycles show the incredible diversity of lifespans in the animal kingdom, from creatures that live just a few hours to those that can outlast entire human generations!

Fun Fact Quiz

Did you know the mayfly lives for just one day?

A. Yes, it has a very short lifespan
B. No, it can live for weeks
C. It lives for months
D. Only as larvae

Answer
A. Yes, it has a very short lifespan

Mayflies have one of the shortest lifespans in the animal kingdom, living just 24 hours as adults after spending up to a year as aquatic larvae. Their entire existence revolves around mating and laying eggs in this brief time!

Humans and Animals: A Special Bond

The History Of Domestication

How did animals like dogs, cats, and horses become such important parts of our lives? In this section, we'll uncover the incredible history of how humans and animals began living together, forming lasting friendships that have spanned centuries.

❖ **Did you know that dogs were the first animals to be domesticated?**
Research suggests that dogs were domesticated from wolves between 20,000 and 40,000 years ago, making them our oldest companions.

❖ **How did cats become our furry friends?**
Cats were domesticated around 9,000 years ago in the Near East, where they helped humans by controlling rodent populations in agricultural areas.

❖ **Did you know that pigs are among the earliest domesticated animals?**
Pigs were domesticated around 9,000 years ago, providing meat, leather, and companionship to early farmers.

❖ **How did horses change human transportation?**
Horses were domesticated around 3500 BC, revolutionizing travel and trade, and playing a crucial role in many cultures throughout history.

❖ **Did you know that goats were domesticated for both milk and companionship?**
Goats were one of the first livestock animals to be domesticated, providing milk, meat, and hides.

❖ **How did sheep provide more than just meat?**
Sheep were domesticated over 10,000 years ago, primarily for their wool, which has been essential for clothing and textiles.

❖ **Did you know that the domestication of chickens began over 8,000 years ago?**
Chickens were initially bred for their eggs and meat, with the red junglefowl being the ancestor of today's domestic chickens.

❖ **How did llamas become integral to Andean cultures?**
Llamas were domesticated in South America around 4,000 years ago, serving as pack animals and sources of wool.

❖ **Did you know that reindeer have been domesticated by some Arctic cultures?**
Reindeer were domesticated by the Sámi people and others in the Arctic, providing food, transportation, and materials for shelter.

❖ **How did elephants become associated with human cultures?**
Elephants have been used in various cultures for labor, transportation, and even warfare, showcasing their intelligence and strength.

❖ **Did you know that ferrets were domesticated to help control vermin?**
Ferrets have been domesticated for over 2,500 years, primarily used to hunt rabbits and rodents.

❖ **How did bees become vital to human agriculture?**
Honeybees were domesticated for honey production and their role in pollinating crops, significantly impacting food production.

❖ **Did you know that fish like goldfish have been bred for companionship for centuries?**
Goldfish were domesticated in China over 1,000 years ago, originally bred for their beauty rather than food.

❖ **How did domestication shape our relationship with animals?**
The process of domestication has led to strong bonds between humans and various animal species, resulting in companionship and mutual support.

❖ **Did you know that animals like parrots have been kept as pets for centuries?**
Parrots were domesticated for their vibrant colors and ability to mimic human speech, making them popular companions.

❖ **How did guinea pigs become pets in many households?**
Guinea pigs were domesticated in South America for food and have become beloved pets around the world due to their friendly nature.

❖ **Did you know that some animals, like the capybara, have become popular pets?**
Capybaras, the world's largest rodents, are often kept as pets in some regions due to their social behavior and friendly disposition.

❖ **How did animal husbandry evolve over time?**
As human societies advanced, animal husbandry practices evolved, leading to improved breeding and care techniques for domesticated animals.

❖ **Did you know that domesticated animals can have diverse roles in different cultures?**
Animals like dogs and cats serve various roles in different societies, from hunting partners to companions and even therapy animals.

❖ **How did the bond between humans and animals evolve with agriculture?**
As agriculture developed, the bond between humans and domesticated animals strengthened, leading to a reliance on them for food and labor.

Fun Fact Quiz

Did you know that dogs were the first animals to be domesticated?

A. Yes, they were the first
B. No, cats were first
C. They were domesticated in the 18th century
D. They were domesticated from deer

Answer
A. Yes, they were the first

Dogs were domesticated from wolves between 20,000 and 40,000 years ago, marking the beginning of a long-standing companionship between humans and animals.

Animal Helpers

Animals play a huge role in helping humans in ways we often take for granted. From service dogs guiding the blind to dolphins assisting in ocean rescues, discover the amazing ways animals lend a helping paw (or fin!) to make our lives better.

❖ **Did you know that dogs can be trained to detect medical conditions?**
Service dogs can be trained to alert their owners to conditions like diabetes or seizures, showcasing their remarkable abilities.

❖ **How do therapy animals improve mental health?**
Therapy animals provide comfort and support to individuals in hospitals, nursing homes, and schools, helping improve emotional well-being.

❖ **Did you know that dolphins can assist in search and rescue operations?**
Dolphins have been trained to locate missing persons in water, showcasing their intelligence and ability to work with humans.

❖ **How do horses help people with disabilities?**
Equine therapy uses horses to assist individuals with physical and mental disabilities, promoting healing and improving mobility.

❖ **Did you know that some animals help in the detection of drugs and explosives?**
Dogs are commonly used in law enforcement to detect drugs and explosives due to their exceptional sense of smell.

❖ **How do cats provide companionship for individuals with anxiety?**
Cats are often used in therapy settings to provide comfort and companionship for individuals dealing with anxiety and stress.

❖ Did you know that monkeys can assist in rehabilitation programs?
Capuchin monkeys have been trained to assist people with disabilities by performing tasks like retrieving items.

❖ How do animals participate in search and rescue missions?
Trained search and rescue dogs are invaluable in locating missing persons in disaster situations, utilizing their keen sense of smell.

❖ Did you know that goats can help with vegetation control?
Goats are often used in ecological restoration efforts, as they can effectively clear invasive plants from areas.

❖ How do elephants assist in conservation efforts?
Elephants are used in some regions for logging and conservation, demonstrating their strength and intelligence in helping humans.

❖ Did you know that parrots can be trained to help people with disabilities?
Some trained parrots assist individuals with mobility challenges by performing tasks like fetching objects.

❖ How do therapy dogs provide comfort in schools?
Therapy dogs are increasingly used in schools to help students with emotional and academic challenges, fostering a positive environment.

❖ Did you know that bees are crucial for pollinating crops?
Bees play a vital role in agriculture by pollinating fruits, vegetables, and nuts, helping ensure food production.

❖ How do service dogs support individuals with PTSD?
Service dogs trained to assist veterans with PTSD provide emotional support and help their owners navigate anxiety triggers.

❖ Did you know that some animals can detect changes in human emotions?
Animals like dogs can sense when their owners are sad or stressed, often providing comfort through their presence.

❖ How do animal-assisted programs benefit children?
Animal-assisted programs in schools and therapy settings can help children develop social skills and emotional resilience.

❖ Did you know that animals are often used in scientific research to benefit humans?
Many medical breakthroughs have been achieved through research involving animals, helping improve human health and well-being.

❖ How do animals help in environmental conservation efforts?
Animals are often involved in conservation programs, helping restore habitats and balance ecosystems.

Fun Fact Quiz

Did you know that dogs can be trained to detect medical conditions?

A. Yes, they can
B. No, only cats can
C. They can only find lost items
D. They cannot be trained

Answer
A. Yes, they can

Service dogs can be trained to alert their owners to medical conditions like diabetes or seizures, demonstrating their incredible capabilities and bond with humans.

Incredible Animal Intelligence

Did you know some animals are so smart that they can solve puzzles, use tools, and even communicate with humans? In this section, we'll learn about the most intelligent animals, from clever chimpanzees to talking parrots!

❖ **Did you know that chimpanzees can use tools?**
Chimpanzees have been observed using sticks to extract termites from mounds, showcasing their problem-solving skills.

❖ **How do dolphins communicate with each other?**
Dolphins use a complex system of clicks, whistles, and body language to communicate, demonstrating their high intelligence.

❖ **Did you know that crows are among the smartest birds?**
Crows have shown the ability to use tools, recognize human faces, and solve complex puzzles, showcasing their remarkable intelligence.

❖ **How do elephants demonstrate problem-solving skills?**
Elephants can work together to overcome obstacles, showcasing their ability to plan and collaborate as a group.

❖ **Did you know that some parrots can mimic human speech?**
Certain parrot species can learn and mimic human words and phrases, showcasing their impressive vocal abilities.

❖ **How do octopuses display problem-solving skills?**
Octopuses have been observed escaping enclosures and solving complex puzzles, demonstrating their remarkable intelligence.

❖ **Did you know that some animals can understand basic human commands?**
Many domestic animals, including dogs and cats, can learn and

respond to commands, highlighting their ability to comprehend human language.

❖ **How do pigs demonstrate intelligence?**
Pigs are highly intelligent animals that can learn tricks, navigate mazes, and even play video games, showcasing their cognitive abilities.

❖ **Did you know that rats can learn from each other?**
Rats are capable of learning new behaviors by observing their peers, showcasing their ability to communicate and adapt.

❖ **How do elephants exhibit self-awareness?**
Elephants have passed the mirror test, indicating a level of self-awareness, as they can recognize themselves in a mirror.

❖ **Did you know that some species of fish can recognize individual humans?**
Research has shown that certain fish can distinguish between different human faces, showcasing their cognitive abilities.

❖ **How do dogs understand human emotions?**
Studies have indicated that dogs can read human facial expressions and respond accordingly, demonstrating their emotional intelligence.

❖ **Did you know that some animals have been trained to assist in search and rescue operations?**
Dogs have been trained to locate missing persons using their keen sense of smell, showcasing their intelligence and training.

❖ **How do chimpanzees display empathy?**
Chimpanzees have been observed comforting distressed companions, indicating a level of emotional intelligence.

❖ Did you know that dolphins can recognize themselves in mirrors?
Dolphins have passed the mirror test, showcasing their self-awareness and cognitive abilities.

❖ How do ravens solve complex problems?
Ravens have been shown to solve puzzles that require multiple steps, indicating advanced problem-solving skills.

❖ Did you know that certain breeds of dogs can learn hundreds of words?
Dogs like Border Collies have been documented to understand and respond to a large vocabulary of human words.

❖ How do orangutans use tools in the wild?
Orangutans have been observed using leaves and sticks to gather food, showcasing their ability to use tools effectively.

❖ Did you know that some animals can pass the delayed gratification test?
Animals like dogs and monkeys can wait for a reward, demonstrating their ability to plan for the future.

❖ How do honeybees communicate the location of food?
Honeybees perform a "waggle dance" to convey information about the direction and distance of food sources to other bees.

This chapter highlights the incredible bonds between humans and animals, showcasing their unique contributions and intelligence. By exploring the history of domestication, the amazing ways animals assist us, and their remarkable cognitive abilities, we gain a deeper appreciation for these special relationships.

Fun Facts Quiz

Did you know that dolphins can recognize themselves in mirrors?

A. Yes, they can!
B. No, they can't!
C. Only some dolphins can.
D. Dolphins don't see their reflection.

Answer
A. Yes, they can!

Dolphins have passed the mirror test, demonstrating self-awareness and advanced cognitive abilities that showcase their intelligence!

Conclusion

We've traveled through jungles, oceans, deserts, and even deep into the animal kingdom's superpowered world! From the record-breaking speedsters to the tiniest but mightiest creatures, we've uncovered some of nature's most extraordinary adaptations and behaviors. There's no end to the fascinating surprises animals have in store for us.

But our adventure doesn't have to stop here. Keep exploring the amazing world of animals around you, whether it's your pet dog, a bird in the sky, or a creature in a nature documentary. Every animal has its own incredible story, and you've just begun your journey of discovery.

Remember, the more you learn about animals, the more you'll see just how awesome and diverse our planet truly is. So, keep asking questions, keep exploring, and always stay curious about the wonderful creatures we share the Earth with!